THE QUEST FOR A FEDERAL MANPOWER PARTNERSHIP

Center for Manpower Policy Studies
The George Washington University

Prepared for the
URBAN OBSERVATORY PROGRAM
NATIONAL LEAGUE OF CITIES

The Quest for a Federal Manpower Partnership

SAR A. LEVITAN
and
JOYCE K. ZICKLER

HARVARD UNIVERSITY PRESS
Cambridge, Massachusetts
1974

Preface

On December 28, 1973, President Nixon signed Public Law 93-203, the Comprehensive Employment and Training Act. Whatever else will follow in the wake of this new legislation, it seems quite clear that the 1973 Act is going to change the cast of characters, if not the play itself, involved in the manpower drama that was initiated in 1962 with passage of the Manpower Development and Training Act.

The United States has developed a wide-ranging set of programs to train, place, and employ unskilled and deficiently educated persons who encounter difficulties in competing for gainful and sustained employment. The programs not only were funded but also designed and initiated by federal officials and the Congress. States and localities were junior partners in manpower activities. In some cases state and local officials were not included in the administration of manpower programs as federal funds flowed from Washington to private citizen groups.

Congress and federal executive officials have made some half-hearted attempts over the years to convert the national manpower system into a truly federal undertaking. Frustrated by congressional opposition to special revenue sharing arrangements for manpower and other social programs, the Nixon administration attempted to decentralize responsibility for manpower programs without the direct blessings of Congress, thereby presumably forcing states and localities to plan and administer the manpower efforts. While these experiments were underway, the congressional logjam in manpower reform was broken in 1973, and the Comprehensive Employment and Training Act was passed, giving state and local elected officials a major role in manpower efforts.

The broad bipartisan support behind the Comprehensive Employment and Training Act indicates that the Congress and the administration have not given up on manpower legislation designed to aid the poorly educated and unskilled to compete in the labor market. Nonetheless, the proposed funding strongly suggests that the fat years for manpower programs are over. Even the staunchest advocates of manpower programs in the Congress have acquiesced to retrenched budgets in the years ahead. To minimize the impact of reduced funding and, it is hoped, to compensate in part for these cutbacks, it is especially important that administrative efficiency be improved to overcome budget reductions.

This study reviews the development of manpower program administration and planning during the nearly twelve years that elapsed between the passage of the Manpower Development and Training Act and the Comprehensive Employment and Training Act. It traces the growth of the federal manpower system and the role played by the federal, state, and local levels of government and private groups in shaping and implementing the system. After reviewing the manpower planning mechanism that developed during the past decade, the several models that made a stab at the delivery of comprehensive or consolidated manpower services are examined. Finally, the authors indulge in some crystal gazing and speculate about the outlook for manpower services under the newly federalized system. While the major concern is with national trends, the study draws heavily on six case studies sponsored by the National League of Cities' Urban Observatory. The reporters for each case study are listed by city:

 Albuquerque: Patrick H. McNamara and Gloria Griffin-Mallory
 Boston: Morris A. Horowitz and Irwin L. Herrnstadt
 Cleveland: John L. Iacobelli and Jan P. Muczyk
 District of Columbia: Robert Taggart
 Milwaukee: Peter Kobrak and Richard Perlman
 San Diego: Robert Peer and Richard Foster

In addition, the Baltimore and Nashville Urban Observatories participated in the exercise, but their reports were not completed at the time this manuscript was prepared. The U.S. Department of Housing and Urban Development, which funds the Urban Observatory program, has left sole responsiblity for the contents of this volume to the authors.

No claim is made that the experience of these cities is typical of developments elsewhere; the diversity in their experiences suggests that generalizations are difficult. But the wide-ranging experiences in manpower planning, programming, and administration reflected in the case studies provide insights into problems encountered elsewhere. The profiles of states and counties needed to fill in the picture of their role in the manpower system were available from a variety of sources, including the staffs of the National Governors' Conference and the National Association of Counties.

The staffs of the Urban Observatories and the individual researchers as well as Lawrence Williams and William Barnes at the National League of Cities' Urban Observatory reviewed the manuscript critically. The study also benefited from the suggestions of Abraham Weiss, Seymour Brandwein, Everett Crawford, and Patricia Marshall of the Department of Labor, Robert Guttman of the Congressional Research Service, Dennis Fargas of the National Governors' Conference, John Torphy of the National League of Cities/U.S. Conference of Mayors, Howard Hallman of the Center for Governmental Studies, William Johnston of the Center for Manpower Policy Studies, Robert Taggart of the National Manpower Policy Task Force, David Snedeker of Olympus Research Corporation, and Christine Evers of Capitol Publications. Beverly Anderson and Barbara Pease helped in the preparation of the manuscript.

Washington, D.C.   Sar A. Levitan
July 1974   Joyce K. Zickler

Contents

The Quest for a Federal Manpower Partnership

Chapter 1

The Evolving Manpower System

The federal manpower system has evolved from a patchwork of intentions and is the product of responses to continuing real and imagined crises. Aside from education, migration, and military policies, direct federal intervention in human resources development dates back to the funding of the federal-state vocational education program in 1917, the establishment of the Vocational Rehabilitation Administration in 1920, and the creation of the United States Employment Service in 1933. The GI Bill, the Employment Act of 1946, the National Defense Education Act, and the establishment of the National Science Foundation illustrate the post-World War II interest in promoting employment and education.[1]

A Decade of Expansion

The evolution of manpower efforts focusing on the needs of the unemployed, unskilled, deficiently educated, and victims of racial discrimination was delayed until the late 1950s. Spurred by the recession of 1957-58, the Senate established the Special Committee on Unemployment Problems at the urging of then majority leader Senator Lyndon B. Johnson in 1959. Its recommendations included retraining the unemployed, liberalizing social insurance, and revamping education programs. At the same time, Senator Paul H. Douglas led a protracted legislative struggle to secure aid for the unemployed and underemployed in depressed areas, which resulted in the Area Redevelopment Act (ARA) of 1961.

The Special Committee's report and the ARA set the stage for the passage of the Manpower Development and Training Act (MDTA) of 1962, whose initial purpose was to retrain adult workers displaced by technological and economic change. MDTA began with a budget under $100 million—small by today's yardstick—and although the worst fears of technological displacement were never realized, the concept of federally funded training and retraining took hold. The next year, MDTA was amended to add retraining programs for unemployed youth, and its budget was expanded. MDTA funds were used not only for institutional and on-the-job training projects but also for the administration, research, and eventually other activities to support the federal agencies.

Of major concern to the Great Society were employment-related problems faced by the poor. The Economic Opportunity Act of 1964 (EOA) created the Neighborhood Youth Corps (a job creation program for poor high school students and dropouts), the Job Corps (a residential program in which school dropouts handicapped by a debilitating environment could be trained away from their homes in surroundings conducive to acquiring a skill), and the Work Experience and Training Program (an effort to help public assistance recipients and other needy people to achieve economic independence). The EOA also created the Community Action Program, which was expected to include locally designed employment and training projects as a part of community action agency activities in poverty neighborhoods. Poor people from these areas were to be employed to help run the programs. The Model Cities program, established in 1965, also promoted manpower projects as part of an effort to revitalize urban neighborhoods.

Other special needs were addressed in 1965 and 1966 EOA amendments. One was to employ the poor in rural conservation and beautification projects—Operation Mainstream. Another effort—Public Service Careers (PSC)—was aimed at creating subprofessional jobs for the poor in the public sector. The "war on poverty" also spilled over into the administration of MDTA through 1966 regulations which required that "disadvantaged" persons comprise 65 percent of the trainees. These disadvantaged persons included unemployed or underemployed people from poor families who were school dropouts, minorities, under 22 years old or over 45, or handicapped. MDTA funds were used to create separate institutional training facilities that were more flexible than those previously available, including skills centers for the disadvantaged and heads of households who could not enroll in regular institutional programs.

The desire to aid the poor also led to the redirection and expansion of the activities of several old-line agencies. In 1965, poverty was added to the list of disabling mental handicaps, thus opening vocational rehabilitation to the poor. The same year saw the passage of the Elementary and Secondary Education Act which provided assistance for schools in areas where the poor were concentrated. A year later, the United States Employment Service (USES) directed its local offices to reorient their activities to serve the disadvantaged. In need of added manpower to fight the war in Vietnam, the military enlisted to help fight poverty by lowering eligibility criteria so that more disadvantaged youths could join the armed services. Finally, 1968 amendments to the Vocational Education Act required that 15 percent of state grants be expended for the disadvantaged.

Manpower programs experienced rapid expansion during the Johnson and first Nixon administrations, peaking in fiscal 1973 at a $5 billion level (Table 1). There were 1.5 million enrollees in the programs administered by the Labor Department during that year (Table 2). The programs experimented with alternative approaches providing a variety of manpower services. Among these services were:

1. Outreach and assessment efforts to locate potential clients, test and counsel them, and refer them to appropriate programs;
2. Institutional training programs and residential facilities providing orientation, prevocational, vocational and remedial skill training, and adult basic education;
3. Subsidized employment opportunities with private employers, such as on-the-job training and preapprenticeship programs, and work experience and public service employment in the public sector;
4. Training allowances, medical assistance, day care, and other supportive services; and
5. Placement, job development, and labor market information programs.

Manpower appropriations also supported experimentation, research, program evaluation, and the collection of labor market data.

Many constituencies for different manpower efforts grew along with the programs and their bureaucracies. Civil rights organizations, labor unions, educational associations, and a host of other public interest groups promoted federal efforts to support their preferences in implementing manpower policies. These diverse organizations tended to oppose encroachment of the federal bureaucracies into their domains while demanding federal dollars. In short, many actors were added to the manpower drama, but their script was largely improvised.

Managing Growth

As Congress and the administration sparked fresh projects to cover newly recognized needs, there was little concern about the duplication

Table 1. Outlays for Manpower Programs (millions).

Program	Fiscal year				
	1961	1964	1967	1970	1973
Total	$235	$450	$1775	$2596	$4952
Department of Labor					
United States Employment Service	126	181	276	331	431
MDTA-institutional	—	93	221	260	358
Job Corps	—	—	321	144	188
JOBS	—	—	—	86	104
Jobs-Optional	—	5	53	50	73
NYC-in-School	—	—	57	58	73
NYC Summer	—	—	69	136	220
NYC Out-of-School	—	—	127	98	118
Operation Mainstream	—	—	9	42	82
Public Service Careers	—	—	—	18	42
Concentrated Employment Program	—	—	1	164	129
Work Incentive Program	—	—	—	67	178
Public Employment Program	—	—	—	—	1005
Program Administration, Research, and Support	8	23	118	143	209
Department of Health, Education, and Welfare					
Vocational Rehabilitation	54	84	215	441	636
Work Experience	—	—	120	1	—
Other programs					
Veterans programs	14	12	19	141	291
Other training and placement programs	8	15	116	277	384
Employment-related child care	26	37	53	141	433

Note: Details may not add to totals owing to rounding.

Source: U.S., Office of Management and Budget, unpublished tabulations.

Table 2. New Enrollees in Department of Labor Employment and Training Programs (thousands).

Program	Fiscal year			
	1964	1967	1970	1973
Total	34.1	833.3	1051.4	1537.7
MDTA-institutional	32.0	150.0	130.0	119.6
Job Corps	—	—	42.6	43.4
JOBS	—	—	86.8	51.5
Jobs-Optional & National OJT	2.1	115.0	91.0	147.5
NYC-in-School	—	166.8	74.4	165.3
NYC Summer	—	227.9	361.5	388.4
NYC Out-of-School	—	161.6	46.2	74.7
Operation Mainstream	—	11.0	12.5	37.5
Public Service Careers	—	1.0	3.6	24.6
Concentrated Employment Program	—	—	110.7	68.8
Work Incentive Program	—	—	92.7	238.5
Public Employment Program	—	—	—	177.9

Note: Details may not add to totals owing to rounding.

Source: U.S., Department of Labor, *Manpower Report of the President, 1973* and *1974* (Washington: Government Printing Office, 1973 and 1974), Table F-1.

and overlap which was developing among proliferating agencies and institutions of the manpower system. However, it was not long before policymakers recognized that if this social experimentation in manpower programs was to be transformed into a continuing effort to alleviate employment and training deficiencies, the fragmented manpower system must be reorganized. But while some administrators attempted to consolidate and rationalize manpower efforts, Congress continued to experiment with new programs to cope with still emerging problems. The Work Incentive (WIN) program was established in 1967 to help (or induce) public assistance recipients to achieve economic independence, and the Emergency Employment Act was passed during the 1971 recession to create jobs for the unemployed. Amendments to many pieces of manpower legislation and changes in the regulations which defined their implementation were made in rapid succession, leaving administrators unable to cope with such rapid growth and change. As a result, their attempts to cope with the changes often added to the confusion.

One of the earliest efforts to coordinate federal manpower programs grew out of Title I of the MDTA, which gave the Secretary of Labor a special position as manpower adviser to the President. A new Manpower Administration was created within the Department of Labor in 1963 with initial responsibilities for the employment service, unemployment insurance, apprenticeship, and MDTA training activities. In time, this agency took over the administration of the Neighborhood Youth Corps (NYC), Operation Mainstream, and Public Service Careers as these programs were transferred from the Office of Economic Opportunity (OEO) to Labor.

A 1964 executive order created the President's Committee on Manpower, chaired by the Secretary of Labor and consisting of fourteen cabinet and agency heads. A similar executive order established an Interagency Committee on Education to coordinate education programs, many of which were closely related to manpower. The committee gathered data about the status of thirty local programs with the goal of helping local sponsors unclog the lines of communications between themselves and federal officials. However, the functions of the committee were duplicated by the responsibility assigned to the Director of OEO to coordinate all federal antipoverty efforts. Similarly, the law creating the Department of Housing and Urban Development empowered it to coordinate all federal programs in urban areas. In neither agency, however, was manpower a top priority, while the Labor Department displayed sustained interest in manpower efforts and a will to dominate the field.

The proliferation of programs made the need for administrative rationalization increasingly clear. Each program had different authorizations, guidelines, clienteles, and delivery mechanisms. At the local level, this often resulted in duplication or gaps in coverage, or in the establishment of programs ill-designed for local needs. Congress recognized the need for a single, comprehensive program that would provide a series of related services to clients and legislated a provision for the coordination of most EOA manpower programs when it added the Comprehensive Work and Training Programs (CWTP) to the EOA in 1967. The authority for the CWTPs lay dormant until experimental comprehensive manpower programs were proposed in 1973. The apparently most promising approach to reform, and the one favored by many manpower administrators and evaluators, called for adoption of a single spigot at the federal level to fund manpower programs. Implementation of the concept required congressional action to consolidate the many pieces of legislation. Although the Nixon administration flirted briefly with a plan to achieve this end without congressional blessing, a compromise was reached with the passage of the Comprehensive Employment and Training Act (CETA).

Even before the new manpower law was enacted, the Department of Labor was able to take steps to improve the operation of the manpower system. On one hand, federal officials attempted to link the various programs and sponsors at the local level in a Cooperative Area Manpower Planning System (CAMPS). In another step, federal officials promoted a series of efforts to consolidate sponsorship of programs at the local level. Foremost of these was the funding of the Concentrated Employment Program (CEP) which was given congressional blessings in the 1967 EOA amendments. CEP's goal was to enhance the employability of persons living in poverty areas by providing them the variety of services they needed. The efforts, in turn, generated some independent attempts by state and local officials to consolidate manpower programs and to apply them to area policy goals, but by and large most of the impetus for changing the manpower system came from the federal level.

Under the Nixon administration, manpower reform took a new direction. One tenet of the administration's "New Federalism" was that locally oriented social programs are best administered by those closest to an area's needs and that local elected officials could best respond to community desires. Decentralization was presumed to involve the shifting of administrative power out of the hands of the program agents, who belonged to a professional bureaucratic cadre, to elected government officials. In 1971, manpower was singled out—along with urban development, rural development, education, transportation, and law enforcement—to be funded under "special revenue sharing" arrangements, which according to the prevailing rhetoric, was a strategy to give power back to the people.

It took almost five years from the time manpower decentralization was first proposed before a new manpower law was signed. During that period, the administration sought to work within existing manpower systems to consolidate authority in state and local governments. Elected officials were prodded to chair local manpower planning committees and to assume sponsorship of community action agencies and Concentrated Employment Programs. In 1970, a manpower reform bill was vetoed by the President in part because it provided for public service jobs. Nonetheless, a year later under the pressures of a recession, the Emergency Employment Act (EEA) was signed. The EEA contributed to the development of local expertise by delegating to governors, mayors, and county officials the prime responsibility for administering this program.

In 1973, with bipartisan backing and active Labor Department cooperation, Congress passed the Comprehensive Employment and Training Act, consolidating under a single law the separate MDTA and EOA funded manpower programs. In addition, it provides for public employment and thereby indirectly extends the Emergency Employment Act. CETA does not signal the end of efforts to reform the manpower system, having left out of the legislation several major manpower programs. The manpower program for public assistance recipients (WIN) and the activities of the employment service were not included, nor were Veterans Administration and other related manpower programs. Incorporation of these programs in CETA was beyond the jurisdiction of the House Education and Labor Committee and the Senate Labor and Public Welfare Committee. Their inclusion would have required encroachment on the preserves of the House Ways and Means Committee, Senate Finance Committee, and the Veterans Committees in both houses and might have antagonized the clienteles of the veteran programs who preferred a separate agency to administer their programs.

Alternative Organizational Schemes

Being the product of prolonged debate, the Comprehensive Employment and Training Act is a compromise. It incorporates the principles of a single source of funds, but only for MDTA and EOA programs, and of consolidated prime sponsorship by state and local governments. CETA embodies many of the demands made for manpower reform over the past decade. However, other alternatives have been proposed that are worth mentioning.

1. Manpower programs could continue to operate as they did before CETA was enacted. Although the proliferation of programs and sponsors made efficient administration at state and local levels difficult, the competition for federal funds among public and private sponsors may have been beneficial. The system developed expertise in manpower and allowed experimentation with various program designs through expanding funds. Indeed advocates of proliferation claimed that because funds arrived in local areas by several different channels, the total outlays rose above the level that might have been attained with a single source. The system also had the advantage of assuring that federally established goals and standards for each categorical program were followed and that the clientele were selected according to nationally designated objectives.

2. At the other extreme is a manpower revenue sharing program as originally proposed by the Nixon administration. Shared revenues were to be made available to state and local governments with few federal guidelines, little oversight, and no federally sponsored programs. Opponents warned that by "putting the money on the stump and running" federal aims and priorities might be ignored.

3. Another proposal has been to create a "superagency" at the federal level to administer all human resources programs. President Nixon, in his 1971 State of the Union Message, proposed consolidation of seven federal departments (excluding State, Defense, Justice, and Treasury) into four: Human Resources, Community Development, Economic Development, and Natural Resources. Under the Human Resources umbrella, manpower programs (including the employment service and unemployment compensation) would have joined with social security, education, and social and rehabilitation programs. Since the President was unable to interest Congress in this proposal, one can only speculate whether the massive bureaucracy created by such a confederation could have effected much change and improvement in the administration of human resources programs.

A unified human resources agency with a single source of funds is unlikely to be realized, and this could be fortuitous for the constituents of manpower programs. Given the relatively small size of manpower funds in relation to the other human resources programs, manpower goals could easily be lost in administering a consolidated human resources program. The employment service, education, social security, vocational education, and rehabilitation programs each have strong vested interest groups which would tend to relegate to low priority the needs of disadvantaged clients. For the poor and minorities to retain a voice in the nation's human resources policy, a separate manpower organization might be desirable.

4. A fourth alternative, and one that could prove complementary to the implementation of CETA, is the refinement of efforts to coordinate manpower and related social service programs. Rhetoric exalting the virtues of interagency cooperation to plan and deliver a full range of social services has abounded. Manpower programs cannot be expected to solve with their limited budgets the family, health, transportation, and child care problems that beset the clients of employment and training efforts. Manpower programs must depend on other agencies to provide these services. Moreover, the services of the training programs not included under CETA—WIN, vocational education, vocational rehabilitation, and veterans programs—specialize in serving clients who otherwise might turn to manpower programs for help.

Instead of struggling to combine all training and social services into a single delivery system, federal policymakers might choose to provide incentives to improve human resources planning. In the past, the nationally designed comprehensive programs and planning schemes suffered from a lack of enforcement teeth or significant financial incentives and ignored local variations in abilities or needs. CETA introduces incentive grants which the governors may distribute for vocational education projects to supplement manpower efforts. The new law also provides for advisory planning councils which include members from all segments of the human resources community. Policymakers will want to continue to build on these linkages and experiment with additional ones.

Funding Arrangements

No matter how the system is organized, federal manpower monies are distributed according to at least seven different legislative formulas. Since to a large extent he who pays the piper calls the tune, it is important to understand these arrangements and their contributions to the development of the manpower system.

1. The oldest form is the matched grant-in-aid, inducing states to

offer vocational education and rehabilitation services. As a strategy, matching grants have the advantage of allowing the federal government to influence the state's mix of services without extensive federal involvement in program operation. In practice, this arrangement has allowed states some freedom to spend money as they see fit, while the federal government is able to watch over their shoulders to see that its priorities and goals are met.

2. In 1933, the United States Employment Service became the predominant state manpower agency. Funds to support USES, as well as state unemployment insurance operations, are allotted by Congress to the states from a special federal trust fund collected from employer payroll taxes. This unique funding procedure has left the employment service in a somewhat anomalous position. Although budget control normally means administrative control, many state employment services managed to operate independently.

3. MDTA was a third variation on the state agency model. Projects were planned by the states and then sent to federal agencies for approval. Except for 10 percent in-kind contributions made by project sponsors, MDTA funding was almost entirely federal. The control retained by the federal government under the MDTA design was somewhere in between the loose grant-in-aid approach and the tight categorical grant system of the antipoverty programs. At the state and local levels, projects were planned jointly by the state employment security agencies—which established occupational need, recruited trainees, and paid stipends—and the vocational education agency—which conducted classes or certified local training sites. Their proposals were in turn submitted to the Department of Labor and HEW, which shared responsibility for approval.

4. The Economic Opportunity Act of 1964 introduced a fourth funding arrangement to the manpower effort—narrowly earmarked categorical grants by federal agencies to local sponsors. In most cases, the sponsors were private organizations dependent upon federal funds which operated outside state or local governments. This approach had the advantage of targeting specific services to designated groups or geographical areas. An accompanying disadvantage was a lack of coordination among categorical program agents, not only with each other but also with other programs and agencies funded through state and local public agencies. The EOA programs represented the zenith of direct federal control over local efforts. Guidelines for each program

were extensive, and each project was contracted separately by the federal government, bypassing both state and local officials. This system of categorical grants stimulated the formation of ad hoc community agencies to sponsor programs and added over 1000 private sponsors to the manpower system.

5. An additional federal funding model has been adopted by the Veterans Administration to support institutional training among recently released military personnel. Federal funds are distributed directly to the individual to use at any facility acceptable under VA guidelines. Except for isolated experiments, this model has not been extended to other groups in need of education and training.

6. A newer method of funding was implemented under the Emergency Employment Act of 1971. Funds were granted to state, county, city, and Indian reservation governments to hire public service employees. The funds were distributed according to a federal formula which took into account the total number of unemployed in the state and the amount of excess unemployment, with the Secretary of Labor reserving some funds for discretionary allocation. The Public Employment Program was still a "categorical" federal program, but it decentralized decisionmaking authority.

7. CETA provides block grants to states and localities with populations over 100,000 by formula and provides for nationally sponsored efforts. Still, CETA is far removed from special revenue sharing which would allow mayors, governors, and county officials virtually complete freedom to design and implement programs. CETA provides for federal approval of the sponsors' plans and federal accountability for service to priority groups.

Carving a Federal System

This brief review of manpower policies and funding arrangements suggests many underlying complications. The passage of the 1973 CETA offers a convenient point from which to review the development of the manpower system over the past dozen years. Today's problems in planning and operating manpower programs are actually old ones, although they may appear new to many governors, mayors, and county officials who only recently have been drawn into the federally initiated manpower efforts to enhance the employability of the poor, the deficiently educated, and the unskilled. New legislation will not solve most of the complex organizational relationships in the manpower system. However, it is the culmination of a decade of experimentation in trying to rationalize the manpower system with planning and comprehensive program schemes. In implementing CETA, both federal and local officials should be mindful of the lessons of the past.

Over the past twelve years, the manpower system has been more national than federal. Washington-based bureaucrats dominated the planning, design, and implementation of the programs and set the pace of manpower reform, from time to time offering incentives to reorganize and redirect the way manpower services were planned and administered. Federal oversight responsibilities have focused on assuring that federal social dollars are applied to nationally identified needs; federal attention to the problems of manpower coordination efforts was primarily to interagency relationships at the national level.

In contrast, states, and especially local sponsors, have had to face the operational realities by serving their local manpower constituencies while simultaneously fulfilling federal requirements. Though local manpower officials normally acted under federal directions, their response displayed wide variation in adapting the federal guidelines. Numerous bureaucracies and constituencies have carved out pieces of the local manpower turf. The local experiences cannot be readily synthesized, but, through a group of case studies, state and local experience with manpower institutions and their implementation of federal directions in planning and programming can be portrayed. An analysis of the local experiences illustrates and illuminates the planning of manpower measures and the delivery systems that localities have developed.

Chapter 2

Manpower Administration: The Pieces of the Puzzle

Over the past decade, the development of the apparatus for planning and delivering federal manpower programs required the involvement of all three levels of government as well as many private agencies. It is, therefore, not surprising that the manpower system earned a reputation of being "fragmented," "disjointed," "confused," and "overcentralized." In general, the leadership in planning and designing delivery systems for manpower services has emanated from the top. Federal agencies designed the programs and, in most cases, supplied the funds, cracked the administrative whip, and steered the state and local agents in the direction of federal goals and priorities. The ability of state and local agents to free themselves from federal dominance or to initiate improvements in the manpower system was limited.

The Nixon administration's proposals to overhaul the manpower system sounded a clear challenge to the state, county, and city governments that were to implement the new order. The philosophy of the administration's manpower revenue sharing was summarized in two generic terms—decentralization and decategorization. To decentralize is to delegate power to the state and local decisionmakers—"where the action is." Decategorization is an attempt to give state, county, and city sponsors maximum freedom of choice in fitting the components of manpower services into strategies to combat their manpower problems. It is an attempt to recognize the uniqueness of local manpower problems.

Two rationales were advanced by advocates of the decentralization of manpower programs. They argued that the cumbersome hand of the federal bureaucracy could be eliminated if local management made the decisions. The main by-product presumably would be more efficient utilization of manpower resources: less time wasted in securing federal approval and less money diverted to national priorities which did not necessarily serve local needs. They also emphasized that by concentrating power in the hands of elected officials, federal dollars would be spent more democratically—the assumption being that elected officials are more responsible than appointees or tenured civil servants to public desires. This viewpoint pervades the rhetoric of "New Federalism."

Prior to CETA, the federal role was dominant in manpower organization, funding patterns, and the institutional arrangements. As the federal decisionmaking role diminishes, one of the most basic questions is whether the states, counties, and cities are prepared to assume a larger role. In other words, what will be the payoff on the federal investment in the state and local manpower institutions? Moreover, will these institutions respond with a manpower system that sweeps away the categorical aspects of present manpower programs and provides comprehensive programs responsive to local needs?

While thus challenging state and local bureaucracies, the federal government will be left with the equally difficult feat of untying the federal apron strings. In the future, the federal government's task will be to avoid meddling with manpower programs, while providing helpful technical guidance and retaining sufficient authority to ensure the realization of congressionally mandated objectives to serve the poorly educated, unskilled, and unemployed.

The View from the Top

The hydra-headed growth of manpower programs with various legislative mandates and diverse funding patterns necessitated a series of additions, consolidations, and divisions within the Department of Labor, which was the federal overseer. As a result, by the end of 1973 the federal Manpower Administration employed over 4000 civil servants, 45 percent of whom worked in Washington and the rest in the ten regional offices. But this is only the tip of the iceberg; program operators, consultants, contractors, and researchers added tens of thousands more to the manpower establishment.

Building a Manpower Agency

Before the enactment of the Manpower Development and Training Act in 1962, the Department of Labor's informal "manpower administration" consisted of a Bureau of Apprenticeship and Training (BAT) to oversee the national apprenticeship program, a Bureau of Employment Security (BES) to administer unemployment insurance and the federal-state employment service, a Bureau of Labor Statistics to keep a count of the labor force and related data, and a new training unit to oversee the manpower programs initiated in 1961 under the Area Redevelopment Administration for depressed areas. The Office of Manpower, Automation and Training (OMAT) was established to carry out some of the Department of Labor's MDTA functions. However, OMAT had no operational duties. As a concession to organized labor's concerns for the regulation of training in apprenticed occupations, the responsibility for MDTA on-the-job training was given to BAT, which was dominated by organized labor. Inasmuch as local employment service offices were to certify trainees, pay allowances, and establish occupational needs for MDTA, the corresponding federal authority was shifted to BES. Later OMAT's name was changed to the Office of Policy, Evaluation and Research (OPER), which was more descriptive of its functions.

In 1963, BAT, BES, and OMAT were confederated to form the Manpower Administration. When the 1964 antipoverty act added the Neighborhood Youth Corps program to the Department of Labor's management responsibilities, a new bureau was formed to oversee it. Each of these bureaus maintained its own regional office and a separate staff and planning section. As more programs were developed under EOA amendments and as the role of MDTA was expanded, the need became apparent for a consolidated agency to encompass all work and training programs. Accordingly, the Department of Labor set up the Bureau of Work Training Programs (BWTP) within the Manpower Administration in 1964. But a combination of bureaucratic resistance to change, the administrative decision to exclude MDTA from BWTP, and the passage of new manpower programs such as WIN prevented real consolidation.

In 1969, the Assistant Secretary for Manpower, Arnold Weber, attempted to centralize manpower programs at the federal level and to decentralize program operations. Authority for the administration of manpower programs was delegated to ten regional offices which reported to the Office of the Deputy Manpower Administrator (now the Office of Field Direction and Management) in Washington. Then in 1973, in anticipation of new manpower legislation consolidating MDTA and EOA programs, the Manpower Administration was reorganized (Chart 1). BAT, the USES, the Unemployment Insurance Service, OPER, and the Office of Administration and Management

Chart I. Manpower Administration Organization, 1973.

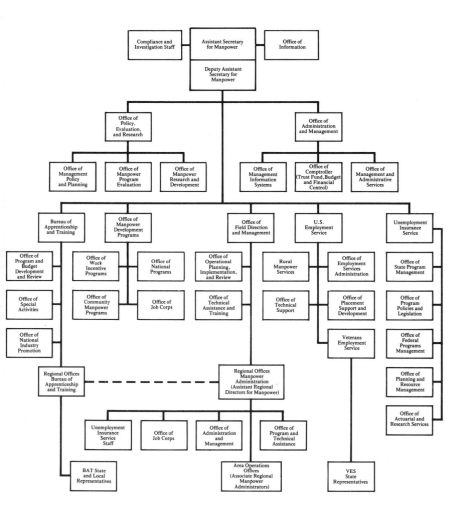

Source: Manpower Information Service, *Reference File* (Washington: Bureau of National Affairs), p. 81:1021.

were retained, and all program administration was consolidated in the Office of Manpower Development Programs. Substantial national direction will continue to be given to the Job Corps and other national programs authorized by CETA and to WIN. However, in the case of programs sponsored by states and localities, the regional offices will have the most significant oversight responsibilities.

The regional offices function as federal line representatives in the field. Under MDTA and EOA, they were assigned funding and monitoring duties, and under CETA they will handle grants to the 500 state and local prime sponsors. These offices will be responsible for broad reviews of the performance of sponsors and will provide technical assistance. As they did prior to CETA's passage, the regional offices will continue to collect data on the activities of the state employment services and WIN programs which along with CETA data will be reported quarterly to Washington.

Although the theory behind a regional management structure is sound, in the past the success of the system has varied among the ten regions depending largely on the abilities of the assistant regional directors for manpower. Whatever its potential, the structure was weakened by poor management in some regions and by the failure to appoint permanent administrators to head the offices. The structure also suffered from legislative requirements which created conflicts of authority and difficulties in coordination. This defect was not wholly corrected by CETA, which funnels money directly to state and local prime sponsors, but will require them to negotiate separate agreements with vocational education facilities, the employment service, or WIN programs for participation in local manpower projects.

Management at the top of the federal manpower organization has focused on monitoring and evaluating program operations, issuing general policy guidelines, orders, and program letters, and establishing priorities, eligibility criteria, and operating standards. Most of the explicit contract management functions were delegated to the regional offices during the early 1970s. Their burden of over 10,000 separate contracts will be reduced to about 500, excluding contracts for national programs under CETA. However, whether the directions and advice came from Washington or from regional offices, the impact on local program operations was more often restrictive than constructive. Success in adapting the programs to local needs depended on the abilities of state and local agents who delivered manpower services.

The State Role

The creation of state manpower offices is a recent development. Over the years, primary responsibility for state participation in manpower programs has rested with the employment security, education, and welfare agencies. In addition, between fiscal years 1972 and 1974, states administered public employment funds under the Emergency Employment Act of 1971. The volume of federal manpower dollars flowing into these state agencies is considerable—nearly $1 billion during fiscal year 1973 for the employment service, WIN, and MDTA, $1.1 billion in vocational education, and rehabilitation funds, and an additional $465.5 million during fiscal years 1972 and 1973 in public employment funds.

However, the state agency most closely associated with manpower efforts has been the employment service, a professional bureaucracy, over which governors, until recently, chose to exercise little authority. The employment security agency, which includes the employment service and unemployment insurance program, is completely federally funded. The United States Employment Service received an estimated one-half of the $851 million in administrative funds expended from the Unemployment Trust fund in fiscal year 1973; the remainder was spent to operate the unemployment insurance program, which paid $4.5 billion from the fund to claimants. With these funds, USES supported 2400 local offices employing over 30,000 interviewers, counselors, placement specialists, occupational analysts, and administrators. Although the primary obligation of the local USES offices is to refer jobseekers to employment opportunities, these offices also prepare state and area labor market reports which have provided the principal source of local labor market statistics for manpower planners other than that obtained from decennial census data. In the past, USES also has been delegated operational responsibilities under several manpower programs. In fiscal 1973, the agency received $202 million to pay training allowances to enrollees in MDTA-institutional training programs and to support an additional 13,750 state personnel involved in manpower programs.

In most states, the governor is empowered to appoint the employment service director who oversees activities throughout the state. Owing to the full federal funding of the employment service, this potential leverage to bring the employment service under state control was often offset.[2] Only within the last several years have some governors begun to reassess their position vis-a-vis the employment service.

Nevertheless, federal influence over state employment service activities is not to be ignored. The state agencies are required to formulate annual plans of service that are presumably subject to approval by the Secretary of Labor. There is, in reality, little critical review since the Department of Labor must veto or approve the entire plan. However, federal officials can use budget allocation pressures to modify employment service operations. Even when the employment service was given additional responsibilities under MDTA and EOA, the state agencies maintained substantial independence from the Washington bureaucracy. As state employees funded by the feds, state employment service officials exist in an administrative never-never land, imperfectly controlled by state houses or Washington.

This independence was not challenged by CETA. The Act suggests that employment services participate in coordinating state agency activities with those of local sponsors and that local manpower sponsors utilize the local employment service offices as delivery agents, as was done in the past. Although the organizational structure of the federal-state employment service and the trust fund grants remain unchanged, federal contributions to state employment services to defray the costs of services to manpower programs are now the responsibility of state and local governments, who may choose to purchase the same services from other organizations or to provide the services themselves.

The influence of federal funding on other state agencies is also limited. Direct federal contributions to education (except for vocational education) are of recent vintage and account for only a small proportion of a state's educational outlays. Federal contributions to welfare are more significant in size, but, like education agencies, welfare agencies are more closely allied with state legislatures and governors than the employment service.

Moreover, state education and welfare outlays dwarf expenditures for manpower. In fiscal 1973, state legislatures appropriated an estimated $29.4 billion and local governments contributed another $27.6 billion for education. Federal aid to education totaled $10.2 billion, with a third distributed to state and local governments.[3]

In contrast, in fiscal 1973, the federal share of the vocational education bill came to $592 million; federal vocational rehabilitation funding added $636 million. MDTA-institutional projects accounted for only

$358 million in training expenditures administered by the vocational education offices. During the same year, state welfare agencies expended over $11.2 billion in public assistance (including federal and some local funds).[4]

State welfare agencies received another $266 million in fiscal 1973 for the WIN program, which is aimed at employing recipients of Aid to Families with Dependent Children. However, these state agencies agreed to let local welfare offices refer potential WIN enrollees to the program, while continuing to provide their supportive services. WIN training was turned over to the local employment service offices and, under proposed revisions in WIN, welfare applicants will be required to go first to the employment service to undertake a search for a job before being qualified for welfare payments.

The Public Employment Program (PEP) was a newcomer on the state manpower scene. It brought the states an estimated $465.5 million to spend on public service jobs by the end of 1973. Many states assigned responsibility for the administration of the program to their personnel offices or civil service commissions, thereby treating it as a revenue sharing program, with little regard for manpower goals. Governors who had state manpower offices, however, used them. As a result, coordination of PEP with state manpower planning varied, with some governors consulting the state's manpower planning committee on the use of the funds; others ignored PEP's potential role in manpower planning.

Rounding out state manpower responsibilities has been the requirement that the governor designate a training agency to exercise contract authority for federal on-the-job training contracts with private employers, unions, and trade associations. Again, the state employment service usually has performed this function. State apprenticeship councils oversee the formal apprenticeship programs operated by unions and employer associations. Like regular state vocational education, apprenticeship generally has remained divorced from other state manpower programs. Wherever the Department of Labor has attempted to develop apprenticeship and on-the-job training programs for minority youth, these largely have been national efforts and have bypassed state institutions.

With the exception of the employment service, manpower has not enjoyed a high priority among state agency activities. Moreover, governors and state legislators have only in the past several years begun to commit themselves to better utilization of their federal manpower funds. The limited interest in manpower to date among state education and welfare agencies has only served to focus attention on the state employment service to speak for state manpower interests. Because CETA will place a portion of manpower monies directly in the hand of the governors, it is possible that more will attempt to reorganize their state manpower efforts and to coordinate new funds with the traditional agencies. However, CETA is likely to make only marginal changes in the activities of these agencies. The influence of the employment services will continue to be considerable, except where governors become active in exercising control over state manpower institutions. State employment services will continue to be the predominant labor exchange, and they will maintain their WIN and apprenticeship duties. It is possible that vocational education agencies will become slightly more active in state manpower since CETA provides governors with some supplementary vocational education funds to be distributed on the basis of the recommendations of local and state sponsors.

Improving State Manpower Administration

With an eye on CETA's mandate that the governors become more active in state manpower, it is important to note a few early examples of state manpower reform. In 1968 California was the first state to make a major effort to coordinate manpower and antipoverty activities. The state law that created the Department of Human Resources Development (HRD), now the Department of Employment Development, was hailed as a political breakthrough because it involved the cooperation of a conservative Republican governor and a liberal Democratic state legislature. More important was the forward-looking nature of the enabling legislation. It provided for combining a wide range of federal and state-funded programs under a single administration. And it called for the pooling of federal funds, regardless of sources, with state funds to create a single account from which the new department could spend according to its own priorities.

This superagency had its weaknesses, too. It lacked responsibility for statewide planning, and its funding was limited. Multiservice centers were established in HRD target areas, where eligible applicants were to be assigned to the case loads of "job agents"—an effort to give the disadvantaged a full range of services. Instead of fostering coordination, the effect was to divide the California employment service into two separate agencies: the traditional placement agency and the minority-run HRD agency for the disadvantaged.[5]

Utah's approach to coordinating state manpower services was to legislate a state Manpower Planning Council in 1969. Because Governor Calvin Rampton believed that manpower planning and operations should be separate functions, the council was given little operational responsibility. Its staff comprises the Division of Manpower Affairs in the State Planning Office.

Notable in the Utah legislation is the provision giving the council the power to allocate resources among state agencies. Although the council took over state manpower planning, the Utah law spelled out further specific powers for the new council: to evaluate budgets, staffing patterns, and activities of state agencies and delivery systems; to approve proposals and modifications in manpower programs; and to review all applications for federal funds.[6] This concentration of power was so offensive to at least one federal agency that it unsuccessfully sought a legal opinion exempting its programs within the state from review by the council.

Although California and Utah represent exceptions, most governors and state legislators were slower in reorganizing their manpower efforts and assuming authority over statewide manpower planning. Despite an invitation from the Department of Labor to governors to designate a representative to serve on joint federal-state planning committees and to adopt whatever leadership position they desired, few governors hastened to respond. Moreover, most governors have reacted slowly to the Intergovernmental Cooperation Act of 1968, which provided guidelines for governors to create substate planning areas for all federal programs.

Lately, gubernatorial concern about federal manpower policy has surfaced as evidenced by lobbying efforts which have sought a fair share of the manpower dollars and a role for the states under New Federalism programs. The Office of Federal-State Relations of the National Governors' Conference and sixteen state offices have promoted state interests not only in manpower but also in social services and community development. In the special case of manpower legislation, political divisions were blurred as governors lined up against the Nixon administration's 1973 administrative revenue sharing proposal, demanding legislation that would outline specific authorities for states in planning and coordinating manpower services.

Under CETA, governors have obtained more control of manpower funds than would have been the case under the manpower revenue sharing plan. However, the best the governors could get was a compromise that allowed local governments to submit their plans directly, rather than as part of a statewide plan, and that gave the states prime sponsorship only in areas—the "balance of state"—not covered by local sponsors. However, governors will receive some additional funds for statewide programs. The law also created state manpower services councils composed of representatives of state agencies, local prime sponsors, the public, business, and labor. The hope is that these councils will coordinate state and local manpower activities, monitor local sponsors' plans, and offer technical assistance throughout the state.

The Local Arena

No matter where the lines of authority for a program begin—federal, state, or local—the delivery of services occurs locally. To cities and counties, the fractionalized nature of federal manpower policies left in its wake a complex maze of funding arrangements, administrative guidelines, vested interests, and client groups. At the local level, organizational lines have been far less precisely defined than intended by federal guidelines or program contracts. Program operations were scattered among an array of public and private institutions which sometimes offered similar manpower services to selected portions of the manpower client population. The cities, in particular, were beset by complicated and sometimes competitive proliferation of categorical programs.

State Agencies: A Local Perspective

Although the extent of their involvement in local manpower activities varies from locality to locality, state institutions are well represented at the local level. The local public employment service offices have the oldest manpower mandate—to counsel, test, and refer applicants to jobs. Under MDTA, the state vocational education board was selected to determine the curriculum and arrange for training and instruction in institutional projects. Local employment security offices were asked to establish the need for training in particular occupations, to select and refer trainees, and to pay stipends. Under the WIN program, the local offices of the state welfare agencies or county welfare departments refer eligible public assistance clients to training, but the training programs are administered by the local employment services. Employment services also have contracted directly with federal agencies to sponsor manpower programs or have subcontracted with the local program sponsors for specific services. Finally, state agencies offer other social services, which must be coordinated with manpower programs if manpower clients are to be adequately served.

Much of the lingering opposition to legislating a greater role for state agencies has focused on their history of a lack of sensitivity to the problems of central cities. For example, the establishment of Boston's first MDTA-institutional projects was delayed by the cautious attitudes of the Massachusetts Division of Employment Security, the Massachusetts Department of Education, and the Boston School Department. These agencies were hesitant to accept training rather than immediate job placement as a method of serving the unemployed, and they preferred to emphasize traditional curricula in the school system rather than vocational instruction. Once underway, Boston's MDTA-institutional training courses were offered in the public schools by state certified vocational teachers. The training sites were scattered but rarely were located in poverty neighborhoods. In 1964, when an MDTA Skills Center was proposed for Boston, the site selected was a vacant school in a white working-class neighborhood. These decisions, which reflected no concern for the reactions or needs of the black community, were made before federal guidelines mandated the use of MDTA training funds for the disadvantaged. It was not until the fall of 1970, after a great deal of pressure from minority groups, community agencies, and the mayor's office, that a second Skills Center was established in a low-income, racially mixed neighborhood. Massachusetts vocational educators continue to refuse to contract with private facilities or to utilize uncertified teachers and have continued to select facilities outside of the low-income minority neighborhoods. As Morris A. Horowitz and Irwin L. Herrnstadt described the situation, disadvantaged black and Spanish-speaking Bostonians in effect have been asked to return to the same classrooms to be taught by white teachers who failed them earlier.

Not all educational systems have done so poorly. In Milwaukee, the education establishment called on the Milwaukee Area Technical College, Wisconsin's largest single vocational education facility, to provide MDTA skill training and adult basic education courses. The college has been successful in reaching disadvantaged and minority Milwaukeans, many of them older students returning to school for training or retraining after an unsatisfactory experience in the labor market. Most of the MDTA and adult basic education students are attracted from the inner city, and even in the junior college courses offered during the daytime, half of the enrollees are minority group members.

According to Peter Kobrak and Richard Perlman, the enthusiasm for vocational education programs is also apparent in the Milwaukee public schools. The school system has offered vocational programs in a few specialized occupations and several cooperative programs, and one high school has served as a comprehensive technical school. However, limited resources allow only the enrollment of a tenth of the city's high school seniors in these programs, and the most highly motivated students normally seize the opportunities. Milwaukee's interest in preparing students adequately for jobs has led to a proposal for an experimental career development center which could combine institutional skill training with more extensive work experience and on-the-job training. In sum, the public education system and the manpower program sponsors in Milwaukee have demonstrated the potentials of a closer relationship between vocational education and manpower in the planning of comprehensive community skill training.

Like the vocational educators and local school systems, local employment service offices have often been accused of not having the will or the ability to serve those most in need. The experience of the Massachusetts Division of Employment Security during the late 1960s exemplified these problems. Between 1962 and 1967, the only additions to the Boston employment service's responsibilities growing out of manpower legislation were the referral of clients to MDTA-institutional courses and the researching and reporting on shortage occupations suitable for training courses. In 1967, the Boston office of the state employment service was called on to provide several additional manpower services. The Human Resources Development program provided new funds to allow the employment service to offer more intensive help to disadvantaged applicants. The Boston office used these funds to create two youth opportunity centers near low-income neighborhoods and to station interviewers in poverty areas. In 1968, the employment service was tapped to provide similar services and to refer welfare clients selected by the local welfare department for training in the WIN program.

But even though the employment service did respond, it had difficulty in establishing its credibility in the minority community. In 1969, when the Concentrated Employment Program guidelines were modified to require the prime sponsors to subcontract with the local employment service for interviewing, counseling, job development, and placement services, the Boston antipoverty agency—Action for Boston Community Development, Inc. (ABCD)—resisted a new subcontract with the local employment service that would have changed ABCD's administrative control of its neighborhood centers. However, an agreement was negotiated that retained the employment service staff at the neighborhood centers in much the same manner as before.

As in many other cities, the minority community in Boston was skeptical of the employment service commitment to give special services to minority applicants. The work of Boston's employment service staff in neighborhood centers and the impact that manpower program obligations and HRD had in reorienting regular offices toward job development and serving the disadvantaged lessened the distrust of the employment service. The remaining lack of faith may be exacerbated by recent federal policy shifts requiring employment service administrators to concentrate on placements rather than on intensive services to prepare them for employment—a policy which best serves those who are able to serve themselves.

CEPs brought local employment service offices into direct contact with antipoverty agencies; the Work Incentive program for public assistance recipients created a manpower tie between employment services and the state welfare agencies. Until 1973, when the Talmadge Amendments shifted the program's emphasis away from intensive services to simple job placement, WIN was intended to provide comprehensive services, including counseling, basic education, skill training, health and day care, placement, and follow-up services to welfare recipients referred by the local welfare agency. Teams of counselors and training specialists were to work with clients on a caseload basis.

As Robert Taggart reported, early WIN experience in the District of

Columbia demonstrated some success in moving recipients of Aid to Families with Dependent Children from welfare to work. The District of Columbia Manpower Administration (a unique administrative arrangement combining the functions of the local employment service and a regional office of the Manpower Administration) operated the program, which provided intensive services to about 600 new enrollees each year. Two-thirds of the enrollees were women, and the program made good use of the local availability of clerical jobs in government agencies by concentrating on basic education and clerical training. The District's WIN found jobs for twice as many of its enrollees as the national average and followed most of them through three months of work.

The city's WIN program was revised in 1973 to give more emphasis to placement and, consequently, is expected to serve ten times as many enrollees. Formerly, the District's WIN did much of its training in-house and had a continuing subcontract with the local technical institute for clerical instruction. Despite the success of that strategy, conformity with federal guidelines will leave little time for training or for WIN teams to buy supportive services or to follow their clients after placement. The reorientation and expansion of WIN has placed it in contention with the city's other manpower programs for public and private job opportunities. Since WIN funding is independent of the Comprehensive Employment and Training Act, it is assured a separate role in the local manpower system.

State vocational rehabilitation agencies operate on the periphery of the local manpower systems, serving the physically and mentally handicapped whose special needs make them ill-suited for conventional skill training. Despite a 1965 vocational rehabilitation amendment that broadened the definition of the handicapped to include poverty, there is little evidence that many local vocational rehabilitation agencies have adapted their programs to the needs of the poor. Moreover, few vocational rehabilitation agencies have sought to coordinate their efforts with other local manpower programs.

The Cleveland Vocational Guidance and Rehabilitation Services illustrates the types of services that can be provided by a vocational rehabilitation agency. Serving the physically or psychologically impaired, this program provides its own educational counseling, testing, training, and job placement as well as the medical and physical rehabilitation services its clients need. The agency also runs a special job training program for youth and a day care center. Despite its overlap with other manpower activities, the program prefers to maintain its independent capability to offer an entire range of services and to fit into the manpower system by accepting clients referred by other programs in the area.

Despite the appearance of autonomy, local offices of state agencies established to deliver employment, welfare, and education programs actually are under state control. The MDTA-institutional and WIN programs were designed to utilize local outlets of these state controlled agencies. An exception was made in the administration of antipoverty programs where the state economic opportunity offices did not have line authority over local OEO contractors. The OEO state offices were limited to providing technical assistance and advising governors on community action agency activities, while the OEO local program agents contracted directly with the federal representatives.[7]

A Local View of a State Superagency

The coordination of state agency activities, as attempted in California and Utah, can have major ramifications in the local arena. An example is San Diego's relationship with the California Department of Employment Development (DED), formerly the Department of Human Resources Development. Because DED operated WIN, the employment service, MDTA-institutional, and on-the-job training (Jobs-Optional) programs, Robert Peer and Richard Foster found it dominated local manpower affairs in San Diego. The employment service is central to DED. And as was the case in Boston, a large part of the local resentment of the state bureaucracy may be rooted in local distrust that the employment service can serve poor and minority groups.

Consolidation of control of the programs in the state DED office has frustrated local DED administrators who have felt constrained from attempting local innovations. Until 1973, the state doled out MDTA slots to the localities, and there was little flexibility during the year in the administration of training programs. Then, an exception was made and the San Diego DED won permission to spend its allotted funds for MDTA-institutional training without being tied to a predetermined number of "annualized slots." Another innovation in 1973 was the use of teams of local DED personnel, counselors, and teachers to select trainees and to follow up on their experience.

The Legacy of the War on Poverty

Beginning with the passage of the Economic Opportunity Act in 1964, the level of manpower expenditures and the number of national contracts for manpower programs accelerated rapidly. Contracts for new programs were made on a project-by-project basis, and this individual selection of rapidly increasing numbers of sponsors left in its wake new public and private agencies receiving manpower funds.

The Act created local antipoverty agencies that were permitted to vie with other local institutions for Neighborhood Youth Corps and Work Experience and Training programs, and, after 1967, for the Concentrated Employment Program, Special Impact Aid, Public Service Careers, and Operation Mainstream funds. The community agencies funded by OEO received monies to run their own manpower programs, and many chose to offer skill training and to establish neighborhood employment offices. The law also established nationally run Job Corps centers.

In some cities, such as Boston and the District of Columbia, a powerful community action agency captured a lion's share of the area's antipoverty manpower programs. The Boston community action agency, ABCD, assumed sponsorship of the NYC Out-of-School and the Work Experience and Training programs. It put CEP dollars to support an "adult work crew" (Boston's version of Operation Mainstream), a public service New Careers program, and orientation centers where entry level skill training was offered. The agency also operated thirteen neighborhood employment centers, mostly with OEO funds, and recruited Boston's Job Corps enrollees. Only the NYC-summer and in-school programs, which were run by the Boston School Department, did not initially come under the ABCD umbrella.

Similarly, in the District of Columbia, the United Planning Organization (UPO) firmly established itself as a major player in the city's manpower system. Like ABCD, UPO was a product of the antipoverty community agency funding. It contracted for sponsorship of all three Neighborhood Youth Corps projects and for the city's Concentrated Employment Program, through which it established five neighborhood centers. In 1972, UPO contracts accounted for four of every ten manpower dollars spent by the Department of Labor in the District of Columbia. The antipoverty funds also gave the city a Job Corps Center and two Public Service Careers Programs, one sponsored by the city government and one by the District of Columbia Manpower Administration.

Aside from direct funding of projects, the antipoverty efforts also affected manpower programs by reorienting, expanding, and creating new uses for MDTA monies. The MDTA had provided for national on-the-job training contracts with public and private employers, and beginning in 1965 these programs were expanded. In 1971 the OJT program was modified to allow program sponsors to offer less formal contractual arrangements with smaller employers and was renamed Jobs-Optional. Sponsors have been diverse. For instance, the Department of Labor had two MDTA-OJT contracts in Boston, one with the antipoverty agency and another with the New Urban League of Greater Boston. Both, in turn, subcontracted with public and private employers. In Milwaukee, the State Division of Apprenticeship and Training administered the program through a local metropolitan association of commerce, while in San Diego, the local office of the state human resources agency had control. In Cleveland, as in most other cities, the employment service eventually took primary responsibility.

In 1968, additional on-the-job training funds were placed in the hands of a newly created organization of private businessmen, the National Alliance of Businessmen (NAB), thereby establishing still another manpower institution with its own program, Job Opportunities in the Business Sector (JOBS). More than 160 cities had NAB-JOBS programs by early 1974. As was the case in Boston and the District of Columbia, local antipoverty agencies eventually were called on to refer clients to fill slots offered under JOBS contracts to attempt to assure the disadvantaged were hired.

The categorical programs that grew out of the MDTA and EOA provide an outline of services which the 1973 Comprehensive Employment and Training Act sought to consolidate under state and local control. However, CETA did not completely eliminate the proliferation of nationally funded categorical projects serving special interest groups, many of whom are eligible for continued support either nationally or locally under the new law. Examples are OEO's programs for Indians, migrant and seasonal farm workers, and the Job Corps.

Not included in CETA are many small and scattered manpower

projects such as those established by the Bureau of Indian Affairs for American Indians, by the Justice Department for prisoners and ex-convicts, and by the Department of Agriculture to employ students in conservation activities. Cleveland, for example, had seven Justice Department funded programs totaling $2.5 million of the city's $50 million manpower budget in 1973. Several other manpower programs for ex-offenders are sponsored by the city's human resources agency, the city's health and welfare department, and the state vocational rehabilitation agency. The District of Columbia has a skill training program at the prison, projects for newly released prisoners which are supported by the Labor and the Justice Departments, and several special programs operated by the city corrections department.

Two special interest organizations have gained a place in local manpower affairs with the help of national funding—Opportunities Industrialization Centers (OIC) and Operation SER (Service, Employment, Redevelopment). By 1973, over 100 OICs had been established. Modeled after the black-run skills training program launched in Philadelphia by the Reverend Leon Sullivan in 1964, OICs sometimes have received funds from city or state agencies, as is the case in Milwaukee where help comes from the state vocational education agency. OICs also have subcontracted with other area manpower programs, as in the District of Columbia, but they are separate manpower institutions. Operation SER, which has concentrated on providing Spanish-speaking persons with language, skill training, and employment services, has similar independence.

CETA will dramatically change the orientation of community-based manpower institutions, because their support must now come from local rather than federal officials. For example, both OIC and SER were firmly enough established in national manpower affairs that the Senate attempted to support their continued categorical funding in the 1973 manpower bill. However, the conference committee report accompanying the final bill only recognized their achievements, and the Act itself only suggests that they and other community groups be given due consideration by local sponsors. Under CETA, the decisions of local sponsors are open to review by state manpower services councils and the U.S. Department of Labor, thereby giving dissenters an opportunity to appeal a local plan. It is not likely, however, that either the state or federal reviewers would intervene in a community decision to discontinue the funding of a SER or OIC project.

The Public Employment Program

The passage of the Emergency Employment Act in 1971 established a new breed of local manpower program sponsors. The elected governments of 212 cities became the prime sponsors for their local Public Employment Programs. In three-fourths of those cities the PEP administration was delegated to agencies unfamiliar with manpower programs—either the city personnel department, other city administrative department, or the office of an aide to the mayor.[8] Because most PEPs operated independently from other manpower programs, they tended to duplicate the services of existing agencies in screening applicants, counseling, job development, and placement.

Nonetheless, PEP was related to other manpower programs. In some cases, like Boston, the extent of involvement of other city manpower agencies was limited. The Boston employment service and the community action agency were asked to refer disadvantaged clients, but these were among some 7000 applicants for 569 PEP jobs. On the other hand, in the District of Columbia, clerical jobs funded with PEP dollars went directly to trainees enrolled in WIN, and other clerical positions were filled with OIC trainees. The District's narcotics treatment agency, vocational rehabilitation agency, and its work release program for convicts also were able to use PEP employment opportunities for their clients. These linkages were not part of any formal planning process, but were developed independently by the city's PEP staff.

The experience of states and localities in planning and administering the Emergency Employment Act has provided preliminary insight into how states, counties, and cities would respond to decentralization of authority for other manpower programs and into what might happen when funds are distributed by a formula rather than through individual contracts. The results suggest that the states and localities can distribute funds as equitably as the federal government. In fact, political considerations may have played a larger role in the portion of EEA money reserved for the Department of Labor than they did for the state and local program agents. In planning the occupations in which to create jobs and the priorities for hiring the unemployed, these EEA program agents generally displayed a sensitivity to local needs. Regional variations in the public service needs and employment problems identified by EEA planners attest to the fact that EEA funds were programmed to local concerns.

Milwaukee's PEP experience demonstrates how rapidly and smoothly city officials could move in putting the funds to work, meeting local public service needs, and hiring jobless people, particularly those in groups disproportionately represented among the unemployed. Aware of pending legislation, Milwaukee's fiscal liaison officer readied a list of projects and positions rejected earlier by the city for budgetary reasons, thereby assuring that no funds would be wasted on "make work" jobs. The jobs selected were diverse in the education and experience required—from public health service nurses to door-to-door canvassers to unearth unsafe housing conditions. Moreover, the participants were equally diverse. Priority was given to veterans, and no special emphasis was placed on hiring the disadvantaged. Yet 11 percent of the participants were welfare recipients, 17 percent were disadvanatged, and almost half were minority group members.

The EEA experience was not completely positive nor completely transferable to CETA. [9] Because the program was implemented rapidly, the agents had little time to carry out extensive planning. Although PEP guidelines were extremely flexible in the early stages, the later proliferation of directives choked off local initiative. Another difficulty, not unanticipated, was the diffusion of planning ability. Often, the planning was done by personnel or civil service offices rather than by manpower planning councils. Manpower planning experience gained, but at the expense of coordination.

Moreover, EEA funds were an addition to regular manpower funding. CETA's public employment program is, at least initially, much smaller, and allocation decisions may not prove as easy since public employment must compete with other manpower strategies. In some cities, Cleveland is one, absorbing the initial cutback in public employment has brought the mayor and city council into conflict.

CETA's public employment provisions closely parallel the language of the EEA. Therefore it seems likely that many PEP sponsors will be called on to continue to administer local public employment efforts. And, under CETA a greater potential for coordination with other manpower activities exists because the new law consolidates in the hands of elected officials prime sponsorship authority for manpower functions once carried out under MDTA, EOA, and EEA. It remains to be seen, however, whether public officials will be eager to forego the opportunity to hire the best qualified workers from among the unemployed in order to provide jobs for the most disadvantaged area residents.

Unions and Apprenticeship

During the late 1960s, concern about racial discrimination in union hiring led to the development of "hometown plans." These plans called for unions working on federally funded construction to agree with the Office of Federal Contract Compliance to increase the percentage of minority workers on their payrolls in order to bring their racial mix more in line with that of the population of the area. In many cities manpower skill training programs have given special attention to the construction trades and crafts in which union membership assures a well-paid job. The hometown plan hiring goals added a new dimension to the local manpower system, but failed to make many significant inroads in construction industry employment. In Boston, Cleveland, and Milwaukee, for example, slow-downs in the economy made it difficult for minorities to gain a larger portion of the shrinking pie. In the District of Columbia, benign enforcement and a lack of local leadership hurt the effort.

Other efforts sponsored by the Department of Labor to place minorities in apprenticeship and journeyman positions have included the funding of fifty AFL-CIO Human Resources Development Institutes to develop jobs and place disadvantaged workers and the funding of over 100 apprenticeship outreach programs. In addition, the Department of Labor has funded the Urban League to sponsor education and counseling for potential minority apprentices in several cities, including San Diego and Milwaukee. In the District of Columbia, two programs to prepare minority youth for apprenticeship were sponsored by labor organizations. One of these, Project Build, was run by a nonprofit training institution with support from the Greater Washington Central Labor Council and the Laborers Joint Training Fund with MDTA funds.

The overlap of union and manpower goals, in part forced by federal equal employment opportunity requirements, has helped make the AFL-CIO a strong proponent of manpower programs. It may be expected to receive continued federal or local manpower support in exchange for union involvement.

Supportive Services

The employment problems of manpower clients often are compounded by poor health, lack of transportation or child care facilities, or other family problems. Some manpower programs were given authority and funds to provide these needed supportive services, but in many cases resources were inadequate and the local program agents had to depend on developing linkages, often unofficial, with other service agencies.

In the District of Columbia, for example, there were eleven separate federal day care programs in 1971, including five that were adjuncts to manpower programs: WIN, CEP, NYC, PSC, and JOBS. Subcontracts from three city government agencies and several private organizations have supported sixty-two program operators who run 120 centers. Because there were many claimants in the city for supportive services, less than a quarter of the 4450 preschoolers in the centers were children of manpower program enrollees. WIN was the only manpower program with a sizable child care budget; 60 percent of the slots used by manpower clients were filled by WIN children.

Health services for manpower clients have been even more limited in most cities than day care arrangements. When manpower programs were fortunate enough to have health service budgets, they usually had to purchase care from existing facilities on a client-by-client basis. The Milwaukee WIN program, for example, arranged for medical examinations. When these showed that over half of the participants were either overweight or anemic or both, medical assistance was provided to some and others were enrolled in Weight Watchers. In the District of Columbia, the CEP and WIN programs referred clients to the public health, the narcotics treatment, or the vocational rehabilitation program.

Unlike training and transportation allowances, which enrollees normally can get directly from the manpower program in which they are enrolled, health, child care, and other social services require sponsors to make demands on social agencies whose limited resources must be rationed among many other clients. The experiences of 1972 summer NYC programs in the District of Columbia metropolitan area emphasize the limitations of relying on other public institutions for health services. Across the country, enrollees in the summer youth program were to be given complete physicals before they started work.

In two of the District's suburban counties and in one city, the public school systems that sponsored the projects took advantage of in-house physicians; other sponsors were funded to purchase adequate health services. In those cases, all enrollees were examined. But the sponsors who relied on public health facilities were able to provide physicals for only 15 percent of their enrollees.

Under CETA manpower sponsors may choose to provide a full range of supportive services. The pressures of limited budgets are likely to force local government prime sponsors to buy or obtain "free" services from local agencies or to use dollars which might be used for training to provide comprehensive services to, perhaps, fewer clients. Because CETA raises training allowances equal to the minimum wage, allowances will become a larger portion of manpower expenditures. Whether public sponsors will be more effective than private sponsors in obtaining comprehensive client services may be an important indicator of CETA's success in encouraging truly comprehensive programs.

Adding Up the Sponsors

The inventory of local manpower programs in any area in mid-1973 showed a variety of public and private institutions scattered in numerous offices, often offering similar services, and supported with all types of federal, state, and local funds. A General Accounting Office report on federal manpower programs in the District of Columbia counted seventy-six private and public program agents providing services at ninety-one centers supported by seventeen separate federal contracts.[10] The city's public schools, vocational rehabilitation programs, and ex-offender programs are not included in the count. Other cities could prepare even longer lists. While CETA shortens the list of prime sponsors considerably, subcontracts with many former program agents may continue the number and variety of actors in the local manpower arena.

The extent of manpower resources and the number of programs did not always correlate with the city's size or needs. Boston's MDTA and EOA fiscal year 1974 budget of $6.7 million compared with the District of Columbia's $9.4 million. But while the District has a slightly larger population than Boston, the estimated number of people with manpower needs was 166,000 in Boston and 130,800 in the District, including both poor and nonpoor persons who will be unemployed or underutilized and in need of employment-related assistance during the year. Political acumen in how to win federal grants may have played a role in the ability of some areas to get a bigger slice of the manpower pie. However, once the available funds were spread over the total universe of need, there was less than $100 per person, a situation which is likely to continue.

Improving City Manpower

Like the states of Utah and California, several cities ran their own experiments on ways to harness their local manpower efforts. New York City was the first. In August 1966, Mayor John V. Lindsay created a city-funded superagency, the Human Resources Administration, to coordinate all human resources projects in the city except those of the traditional education system. Under its wing was the Manpower Career Development Agency to oversee New York's manpower programs.

Because of the city's unequalled size and the diversity of its interest groups, New York's experience does not apply to other metropolitan areas. Partly owing to problems of size and complexity, the new agency shunned operational responsibilities, choosing instead only to plan and manage the overall program and subcontracting operations to a vast array of sponsors. One of the outstanding features of the New York system was the creation of eleven regional manpower training centers throughout the city. The decentralized system also involved twenty-six neighborhood centers and utilized twice that many local welfare centers. The local employment service, the state vocational rehabilitation department, the city board of education, the City University of New York, and many others participated in the delivery of services. This arrangement had its weaknesses too. Because the New York manpower planners were removed from operations, often they were unable to evaluate realistically the manpower needs at service centers and frequently could not exercise line authority over the centers.[11]

Perhaps Cleveland offers a more typical example of early efforts to improve the manpower system at the city level. In September 1968, the city council, at the urging of the newly elected Mayor, Carl Stokes, created a new Department of Human Resources and Economic Development (DHRED). The department was to consolidate the management of the city's manpower programs and to use economic development funds to promote business growth. A planning function was added in 1969 when the mayor designated the department director to head the local manpower planning committee.

The consolidation of Cleveland's manpower planning and administration under a city umbrella agency fell short of Mayor Stokes' original goals. As of late 1973, the Manpower Division of DHRED was responsible for administering only a handful of the city's programs. Even the director of the city's public employment program did not report to the manpower division commissioner. Moreover, the city's manpower planning council, which also functions under the mayor's auspices, works independently of DHRED. The DHRED manpower commissioner can make recommendations to the planners, and the DHRED director is a member of the council, but the planners and administrators have continued to operate under separate roofs.

CETA was intended to improve chances for coordination by giving elected officials the authority to shift manpower funds among clients, services, and delivery agents as they see fit. A number of obstacles remain, including the continuation of nationally funded manpower activities and the possibility that statewide manpower activities will not be sufficiently integrated with the local efforts. With a plethora of local manpower institutions built up over the past dozen years, each fighting to retain their piece of the manpower pie, the local manpower arena may continue to be as fractionated as in the past.

The Counties and Manpower

Until recently, county manpower institutions were rare. The injection of manpower funds into the War on Poverty was channeled toward the problems of the central cities. Even more densely populated urban counties were often ignored as scarce program dollars were concentrated in the ghettos; where countywide manpower projects did exist, they were largely rural programs. In fiscal 1969, rural areas were found to receive a proportion of manpower and vocational education funds that was only half their proportion of total population. In contrast, they received funds for traditional elementary and secondary education programs greater than their share of the population.[12]

Because counties traditionally have been administrative arms of the state, few have received federal dollars directly. Their major activities related to manpower have been the administration of schools and state welfare assistance. The most common form of county government today is the county commission, which has both legislative and administrative responsibilities.[13]

The development of county manpower expertise has lagged even behind the slow pace in states and cities. A few counties were able to form manpower planning councils under the state auspices, but the Department of Labor almost always turned down county requests to undertake planning independently of the governor. Although counties were able to attract manpower dollars from EOA and MDTA budgets on a project-by-project basis, the first full-fledged inclusion of counties in manpower program operations came with the 1971 Emergency Employment Act, which created 368 county prime sponsors. About the same time, the Department of Labor began to consider the possibility that counties would become eligible prime manpower sponsors if an equitable distribution of manpower revenue funds were to become mandatory. Late in 1971, the National Association of Counties received a grant from the Labor Department for research on county manpower. But not until late 1973 were funds committed to create actual planning capabilities in large counties. Under CETA, most counties will be starting from scratch both in planning and administration of manpower programs.

An alternative to the division of manpower programs among cities and counties is a metropolitan form of government. One of the oldest metro's, Miami-Dade County, Florida, took over sponsorship of most area manpower programs from the local community action agency in 1971. A Human Resources Administration was created within the county manager's office and its manpower division has managed the major manpower projects, except those funded by MDTA. The planning staff also is part of the same organization. Another form of joint city-county government is the Council of Governments (COG). The Mid-America Regional Council, for example, involves 106 cities and eight counties from two states in the Kansas City metropolitan area. This COG, however, has done only regional planning. Nevertheless, like the metro, it exhibits an areawide approach to improving manpower programs and is perhaps close to the idealized notion of labor marketwide planning.

Promoting Interest in Manpower

It was inevitable that the growing manpower establishment would develop its own interest groups. At the early stages of the manpower reform debate, the voices of the private sponsors were the loudest. Mayors were at the forefront of active public officials, counties received little attention, and employment service officials—not governors— often represented so-called state manpower interests. Within the past two years, however, the counties have shown their muscle, and some governors have managed to shake off the "employment service image."

The Department of Labor provided support for manpower staff to work with the public interest groups representing state and local elected officials in the Washington planning and legislative processes. In 1969, the first contract went to the National League of Cities/United States Conference of Mayors (NLC/USCM). The initial goal was to interest city executives in manpower efforts and to provide staff assistance. The National Association of Counties' (NACo) Research Foundation received a similar grant in 1971, and in the following year a Governor's Advisory Manpower Policy Project was funded under the auspices of the National Governors' Conference (NCG).

All three manpower projects have promoted information exchanges among their constituents and with Washington policymakers via meetings, publications, resource handbooks, technical assistance, and on-site visits. While leaving the actual lobbying to the professionals in the parent organizations, the manpower projects promoted the interest and supplied the research necessary for elected officials to articulate their position on manpower reform. In fact, one significant reason that CETA did not include a metropolitan approach to manpower program sponsorship was the balanced strength of each lobby.

All three manpower projects consulted regularly with congressional committee staffs and U.S. Department of Labor policy planning staffs concerning legislative proposals and administrative regulations and guidelines. With the enactment of the new manpower law, the staffs of these projects have helped state, county, and city planners review draft guidelines and regulations and have continued to provide training and assistance in implementing their manpower programs.

Federal funding of special interest groups is not unprecedented. The Interstate Conference of Employment Security Agencies was formed in

1937, and its secretary is paid by the state employment services from their federal trust fund. For many years it was the most visible of the manpower lobbies and promotes a dominant role for the state employment services in state and local manpower programs. Grants to encourage the manpower involvement of local labor groups have gone to the AFL-CIO since 1968, and the union's leadership has become a staunch proponent of public employment efforts. OIC and SER received Department of Labor funds as well, and they lobbied for continued separate funding under CETA. A final interest group, the American Vocational Association (AVA) was also active in the CETA debates. The AVA attempted to preserve the role of the vocational education establishment in institutional training. The vocational educators succeeded only in getting a consolation prize earmarking 5 percent of Title I CETA funds for use by governors to supplement vocational education projects.

Making Sense Out of the Manpower System

Checks and balances in the manpower system have been difficult to define because power has been distributed unevenly among the various governmental levels. Policymaking and budgetary authorities have been concentrated at the top, making the Washington bureaucracy predominant in the partnership. State agencies administer a sizable portion of closely related human resources funds, like welfare, social services, vocational education, and rehabilitation. The public employment service has been the most influential in state manpower affairs and, perhaps, in many localities as well.

The greatest diversity of manpower efforts has occurred at the local level where services are delivered. Local relations between state, local, and private manpower agencies have ranged from hostility to mere coexistence to friendly cooperation. And, despite often diligent manpower efforts, most agencies were able to make only marginal improvements in the lives of clients.

When states and cities made early attempts on their own to improve manpower planning and management, they quickly encountered the limitations of the system. Manpower efforts, strictly defined, were bounded by several distinct pieces of legislation. Each law had unique funding and institutional arrangements, and programs had separate guidelines and regulations. These problems made the realization of a decentralized and decategorized manpower system infeasible and precluded the development of a coordinated "human resources program." The lower levels of the professional manpower bureaucracy, and even elected state and local officials, could not change federal guidelines or shift power among manpower institutions without the help of the federal establishment.

As the system matured, the need to make sense of the manpower system intensified. The federal response took two routes. One was to require local sponsors of federal manpower programs to sit down, if not reason, together and to plan program coordination. The other route was to consolidate and coordinate the delivery of manpower services by the operating institutions so that manpower clients were provided comprehensive manpower services. Since these goals of comprehensive manpower planning and delivery of services are central to the Comprehensive Employment and Training Act, a closer look at earlier federal efforts can perhaps lend further insights into the role of manpower planning and management in manpower reform. What does the evolution of the planning system, officially designated as the Cooperative Area Manpower Planning System, tell about the capability of a federal-state-local planning mechanism? What do the experiences of the community action agencies, the Concentrated Employment Program, and the pilot comprehensive manpower programs suggest for the future of manpower programming? What have state, city, and county governments learned as they responded to federal initiatives to consolidate authority for manpower programs with public sponsors? In brief, what does past experience indicate about the outcome of manpower reform under CETA?

Chapter 3

Manpower Planning: Coordination on Paper

Social Planning and Measurement

One approach to overcome the complexities of the federal manpower system was to create a federal planning mechanism which, it was hoped, would design a coordinated national manpower plan based on state and local plans. Despite some lingering fears that government planning could undermine a democracy, proponents have claimed that social planning is necessary if government is to allocate scarce resources and achieve optimal investments of the tax dollar.[14] It is axiomatic in implementing social programs, including manpower programs, that the available resources are inadequate to provide for all needy clients, and the efficient utilization of resources is, therefore, essential. Though planning has gained respectability in the setting of federal social policy, it has its critics who contend that it constitutes idle gazing into a crystal ball—a fruitless effort with little impact on the status quo. The detractors assert that "planning" is a camouflage for make-work activities which rarely result in the actual implementation of social policies.

This ideological view of planning ignores reality. In real life, a multitude of planning practitioners exist; some—like Molière's hero who was unaware that he spoke prose all his life—are oblivious to the fact that what they do is planning. The legislative process, for example, is planning. Problems are identified; alternative bills are proposed and debated; hearings are held; votes are taken. Whether they acknowledge it, members of Congress are responsible for setting national priorities and outlining attacks on social ills.

On the executive side, there is more readily identifiable planning taking place in the preparation of the annual federal budget. The budget process involves months and years of analysis by the President's Office of Management and Budget and the other executive agencies. The results are assessments of the most politically acceptable and sometimes most effective means of investing tax dollars during the next fiscal year to yield the desired economic outcomes. Despite attempts to conceptualize and glamorize the budgetary process, one astute observer noted that it remains "simply a common sense approach to decision-making."[15]

Within each budgeted program, there normally is enough flexibility to permit resources to be manipulated administratively. Congress rarely spells out instructions for implementing a program. It leaves to the executive branch the responsibility for establishing guidelines, choosing acceptable sponsors, and targeting eligible groups for service. Manpower programs (except in 1971 and 1972) were blessed with bipartisan support, possible because Congress was content to indicate broad goals, leaving much of the nuts and bolts planning to federal manpower administrators.

To plan effectively policymakers must measure both needs and the results of efforts, and both requirements pose a major challenge to the social planner. Establishing the magnitude of need for manpower efforts involves identifying the poor, the handicapped, the undereducated, and the unskilled—just to name a few of the characteristics that establish eligibility and define the total "universe of need." An essential part of the methodology is the arbitrary setting of a standard—family income or years of school completed—below which the needy are found. Rarely is there any consensus about the most deserving groups, and, whoever the recipients are, there invariably is controversy about program accomplishments and shortfalls.

Once those requiring assistance are identified, another thorny problem confronts the social planner. Is aid best directed to those with the most deep-seated social ills or at those who may require only brief and less costly help? Even more difficult is the search for the institutional and individual roots of social problems and the design of alternative strategies for dealing with them. Social programs do not lend themselves to precise quantitative measurement owing to the influence of many intangible variables. The greater the importance of the factors defying measurement, the harder the task of determining the true effectiveness of alternative strategies. The addition of quantitative measures to the social planner's tool kit has not simplified decisionmaking as value judgments remain a controlling consideration. The emphasis on quantification has contributed, however, to a sharpening awareness of the complexity of social problems and the difficulty in applying available data to the measurement of social objectives.

The search for a clear definition of need, the determination of

problem areas, the development of alternative strategies, the design of
social services, and judgments about the performance of social institutions are all obviously part of a planning cycle. Although many analysts
have been able to define the steps in the planning process, few can
boast that their advice has been followed. Nonetheless, planning has
become popular as a potential way to grease the gears of many social
efforts.

The Manpower Planning Structure

By 1967 the federal manpower system had become a complex tangle
of relationships among all levels of public and many private institutions. Planning was carried out through the budget process and via
contractual arrangements with a multitude of program sponsors. The
Departments of Labor and of Health, Education, and Welfare shared
the responsibilities for the Manpower Development and Training Act,
and although there was friction between the two departments about
their respective roles in administering the manpower program, they
were agreed that planning and budgeting authority would be concentrated in national hands. The Office of Economic Opportunity's reins
on its many antipoverty sponsors were not as tight.

The initial impetus for giving a systematic form to the way manpower
programs were planned and budgeted came from the feds—who, of
course, had created the tangled maze of contracts in the first place.
They combined their experience with MDTA budget planning and
their desire for interagency cooperation to produce a planning system
that was compatible with national domination of the planning and
budgeting process.

Initial Efforts

The need for some form of federal-state planning was inherent in the
Manpower Development and Training Act of 1962. The legislation
obligated both the state employment services, whose guidelines flow
from the Department of Labor, and the state vocational education
agencies, which receive grants-in-aid from the Department of Health,
Education, and Welfare, to share responsibility for carrying out the
legislation. Moreover, the funding of manpower training represented a

new form of grant-in-aid under which, initially, federal approval was given on a project-by-project basis. even when this was modified and states received monies distributed on the basis of a federal formula, the states still had to design projects within the federal guidelines in order to get funds.

The architects of the legislation anticipated that manpower advisory committees at all three levels of government would be formed to do planning and to create a bureaucratic linkage, however tenuous, between the Departments of Labor and of Health, Education, and Welfare. A National Manpower Advisory Committee, chaired by a leading academic authority on manpower, Professor Eli Ginzberg of Columbia University, was appointed to integrate state planning with national goals and perspectives.[16] Staffed by Labor Department personnel and with its agendas set by the Manpower Administrator, the committee turned out to be little more than a sounding board for manpower training policies proposed by the Department of Labor.

Originally, MDTA merely encouraged, but did not require, the establishment of manpower advisory committees at state and local levels. The USES and its state affiliates were given the responsibility to encourage the formation of the committees, but little action was taken until the 1964 MDTA amendments authorized the Secretary of Labor to establish the committees. When the state and local manpower advisory committees were finally set up, they were directed to review project proposals rather than take on manpower planning functions. The state and local committees were made up largely of representatives from the professional manpower bureaucracies. Business and labor participation failed to materialize. Local committees experienced some of the same problems that were to continue into the CAMPS effort: connections with the governor were weak, interest in planning could be maintained only as long as uncommitted funds were available, and the employment service often dominated the committees by default owing to the lack of interest by other members. In brief, the committees were too often merely window dressing, and they rarely affected program operations.

The inducement to have these committees participate in the planning process surfaced first in a 1965 MDTA amendment sponsored by Senator Jacob Javits. The measure delegated to the states the authority to review and approve institutional projects costing less than $75,000 annually. Advance planning by the states with federal approval at the beginning of a fiscal year thereby allowed the states to set up projects during the course of the year without having to submit to a time-consuming federal approval process for each project. A second incentive for state planning was found in the 1966 administrative decisions to redirect MDTA programs toward upgrading the skills of disadvantaged workers. The Departments of Labor and of Health, Education, and Welfare outlined for the states the policy guidelines and reviewed their intentions for implementation. [17]

Whatever the incentive, the manpower advisory committees began to prepare written statements of projects and budgets—the so-called MDTA plans, which were compiled into state plans and, in turn, into a National State Manpower Development Plan. There was no real evaluation of this planning process, but the idea of coordinating all manpower programs via federal-state-local planning committees was so appealing that the Manpower Administration proposed they expand their efforts beyond MDTA.

The CAMPS Umbrella

In March 1967, seven agencies of five executive departments reached an agreement to form an area-state-regional-national committee structure to voluntarily coordinate manpower planning. Signatories included the Department of Labor's Manpower Administration; the Department of Health, Education, and Welfare's Office of Education Bureau of Adult and Vocational Education, Welfare Administration, and Vocational Rehabilitation Administration; the Office of Economic Opportunity; the Department of Commerce's Economic Development Administration; and the Department of Housing and Urban Development. Later the Departments of Interior and Agriculture, the Civil Service Commission, and the Environmental Protection Agency were added.

The key word was to be coordination. The formal agreement creating the new planning system described the need for a Cooperative Area Manpower Planning System:

> Federal legislation dealing with the complex of manpower problems and human resources development enacted in the past five sessions of Congress cannot be fully effective in the absence of interagency coordination, since these programs cut across departmental and agency lines both in the Federal sector and at State and local levels. The services provided by manpower and related

programs require maximum feasible coordination of government action; both in the planning stage and during program operations.[18]

The CAMPS coordinating committees were first formed in 1968 in sixty-seven major labor market areas, in each state (and two territories and the District of Columbia), in each of the eleven regional offices of the Bureau of Employment Security, and at the national level. In three years, the number of area committees increased to more than 400.

The original state and area CAMPS committees included agency delegates and one person from the mayor's or governor's office as voting members. Community, business, and labor representatives were sometimes invited to attend, but they could not vote. At the regional and national levels, the CAMPS coordinating committee members were drawn entirely from federal agencies. Initially, few governors and mayors seized the opportunity given them by the interagency agreement to assume "whatever leadership they deemed appropriate" of these committees. Most committees remained agency-dominated until the entire system was remodeled in 1972.

The long list of federal agencies signing the CAMPS agreement is somewhat deceiving. Although the committees were to be formed of agency peers, the Department of Labor was more equal than the others. Area and state committees were chaired at the outset by the public employment service directors, regional committees by the director of the Manpower Administration's regional executive councils, and national committees by the Manpower Administration.

The primary operational function of the state and local CAMPS committees was to draw up an annual plan that would receive the national office approval necessary to allow the state vocational education agency and employment service to carry out MDTA-institutional training projects. Other manpower activities (including those sponsored by the Department of Labor) could not be decided by the plan, and the committees were not motivated to go any further than inventory those other efforts and present their budgets for the coming year. The national CAMPS plan was a summary of the manpower expenditures of all the federal agencies participating in CAMPS. It was compiled from regional summaries which, in turn, were the stapled product of state and local CAMPS plans. These plans rarely were reviewed and they served little purpose, other than to fulfill the requirement of the Executive Order which created CAMPS.

The state and area CAMPS plans were largely descriptive, providing a narrative of economic conditions, manpower problems, and available program resources. Because the overall goal of CAMPS was to eliminate as much overlap as possible in state and area programs, the committees' most significant duty was to demonstrate how the offered services could be coordinated. This exercise was, however, destined to be futile and frustrating. The committees were to outline program goals, priorities, and performance schedules and to evaluate the relationship of resources to needs, but they could not effect changes in the flow of federal dollars. With the exception of MDTA, for which CAMPS committees took over the manpower advisory committees' responsibilities to set funding priorities, the CAMPS committees had scant authority to follow up on the impact of the programs or to evaluate the performance of the sponsors.

The Department of Labor supplied each committee an annual outline of the information to be included in the plans. This contributed further to CAMPS dependency on the Department of Labor and detracted from the original goal of interagency coordination. Even the data on manpower needs and economic conditions included in the plans originated with the Department of Labor or affiliated agencies. At the state and local levels, the employment service usually was the best source of that data, since that agency had been assigned data gathering tasks for MDTA projects. Therefore, the state and area committees' staff functions were housed in employment service offices and, in Washington and the regions, in Manpower Administration offices.

But, CAMPS' greatest weakness was the looseness of its structure. The guidelines specified that no signatory would relinquish any administrative authority over its programs. Since the function most significant to state and local sponsors, allocation of funds, remained outside the domain of CAMPS committees' work, the agencies had little to gain by active participation in CAMPS. As for those agencies that funded overlapping programs—Labor, HEW, and OEO—they already had staked out their territories for operations and generally were careful not to get in each other's way. Therefore, as long as needs were greater than allocations and with agencies not having to compete for funds, the so-called CAMPS' planning process was more a make-work project than real policy formulation.[19]

Milwaukee's CAMPS' experience in the 1967-1972 period is typical. The city's first CAMPS committee was composed entirely of federal manpower program directors and chaired by the director of the employment service. Over the years, membership was expanded to include local manpower agencies and the chairmanship was rotated. However, researchers Peter Kobrak and Richard Perlman found that in Milwaukee, as in most CAMPS areas, the meetings were "wheel spinning sessions." Attendance waned and members complained that they spent most of their time not acting, but reacting to federal forms.

If the committees could do little to change the way funds were distributed and programs operated, they were able to make several small, but positive, contributions to the future course of manpower policy. As irregular as attendance may have been, CAMPS committees were one of the few places where state or area representatives of federal agencies could be found in one place at one time. Even if they could do little operational planning, the meetings at least offered an opportunity to exchange information. State and local CAMPS committees also provided a point of departure for state and city attempts to coordinate manpower programs. Granted, not many states and cities addressed the problem until the later days of CAMPS when the Department of Labor gave them a push by providing funds for manpower planning personnel and offering mayors and governors leadership of the committees. Nevertheless, states, such as Utah, and cities, such as New York, found that CAMPS committees were a convenient base on which to start building local coordination efforts.

Funding Staffs

Complaints from state and local participants about their committees' administrative and financial burdens surfaced almost immediately. Acting on the assumption that big brother knows best, the federal officials who had created the state and local committees also assumed primary responsibility for maintaining them.

The first concrete step to bolster the capabilities of the state and local CAMPS agencies occurred in 1968 when the Bureau of Employment Security authorized its state and local affiliates to provide staff support from MDTA funds. Each state was allocated two positions, and one position was allocated for each of the sixty-seven planning areas (the major labor market areas). The newly designated "planners" were added to employment service personnel rolls, and they were assigned to the local CAMPS chairman, who usually was the director of the employment service. Staff duties included preparing minutes of the meetings, collecting participant information, distributing reports, assembling data, and recommending modifications to the CAMPS plans.

In anticipation of the proposed decentralization of manpower authority to states and large cities, the Secretary of Labor also made grants for CAMPS staff available directly to mayors and governors to encourage them to participate in the federal efforts that were then being made to decentralize manpower programs. By fiscal 1973, fifty-five states and territories, 126 cities, four counties, and one council of governments had received MDTA monies to support manpower planning staff members. In addition, nineteen Indian tribes and forty cities with a large proportion of Spanish-speaking residents got staff support from the Secretary of Labor's national projects funds. Altogether, the funding came to $18 million and paid for over 1200 full-time and part-time manpower planners.

The size of planning staffs varied in 1973 from over thirty persons in New York State to as few as three in Wyoming; most states employed between eight and fourteen people. Cities tended to have fewer positions, usually between two and eight, although larger cities had as many as fourteen staff members. This new breed of manpower planners typically were recruited from the ranks of economists, public administrators, and other urbanologists. They are typically assigned to the executive office of the governor or the mayor. Under CETA, many positions will become part of state and local civil service.

Eventually, the Department of Labor began to expand the coverage of planning grants to all cities or counties with population in excess of 150,000, and then in excess of 100,000, to pave the way for the prime sponsors to be included under CETA. Many of the counties that received planning grants for the first time in 1973 or 1974 were contiguous to cities with already existing planning agencies. Under the eligibility rules established by CETA, as many as 500 planning jurisdictions are possible, and as many as nine may be funded in a single Standard Metropolitan Statistical Area (SMSA). Although CETA provides a financial incentive for multijurisdictional planning, proliferating and apparently duplicative planning agencies may, like manpower programs themselves, soon need a planning agency to coordinate their activities.

CAMPS: A Vehicle for Decentralization

Having funded state and local staffs, Department of Labor policy-makers used the planning system to initiate steps toward decentralizing manpower activities. The first significant shift was to pull elected officials into the manpower arena by formal means. Accordingly, the fiscal 1972 planning guidelines designated state and local elected officials, not professional bureaucrats, as responsible for drawing up and approving the plans. The second step was taken when the Labor Department instructed local planners to draw up their fiscal 1974 plans for MDTA and EOA programs according to local priorities and granted them the opportunity to recommend to the regional offices the allocation of funds for their communities.

State and Local Councils

On the state level, the state manpower planning councils, which were authorized in 1971, were assigned the responsibility for submitting statewide plans. The goal was to force the governor to accept the responsibility for the state manpower plan or at least to designate a responsible official. By 1973, governors of twenty-eight states had moved manpower planning into the executive office; twelve others had state planning agencies or included the planning function in a human resources department.[20]

Although the nucleus of the state planning councils continued to be the representatives of state agencies who sat on CAMPS committees, membership was considerably broadened. Business and labor leaders, local elected officials, and manpower client representatives nominated by interested constituent groups were added to the voting membership of most state councils.[21] CETA retains similar membership requirements for its state planning councils and adds a state manpower services council to the governor's responsibilities to review local plans and monitor the integration of state services with local efforts.

The gubernatorial responsibility to plan for areas of the state not covered by local planning councils mandated by CETA was first outlined in the 1971 CAMPS revisions. By the end of 1973, all but one state had formed area councils, called ancillary planning boards. Although the creation of these planning boards formally included all areas of the state, the boards made only small contributions to statewide planning and normally were dominated by agency representatives. The activities of the staff assigned to area boards by state councils created the illusion of local planning, if not the substance.

Many state CAMPS "plans" were little more than a stapling together of local plans and descriptions of anticipated state agency activities. With few categorical programs operating outside metropolitan areas, state plans focused on allocating MDTA funds and, in some cases, public employment funds and on reviewing expected employment service and welfare agency efforts. A few states had no local councils at all; in these, state councils prepared only a state CAMPS plan.

The first statewide plans were those submitted for fiscal year 1974 by New Hampshire, South Carolina, and Utah, a result of their designation in 1973 as pilot comprehensive planning projects. Utah, which began to consolidate manpower planning authority in 1969, offers one example of successful resolution of state and local conflicts to allow true statewide planning. Although Salt Lake City had been eligible to form a manpower planning council, the mayor chose to remain uninvolved in social welfare programs. However, when the state proposed a pilot comprehensive manpower project in 1973, the new mayor was unwilling to allow the state to assert its manpower planning authority on a statewide basis without a stronger role for the city's manpower planning council.[22]

The pressure on the state manpower planning council to give Salt Lake City a special voice in the statewide plan was an element in the decision by Governor Calvin Rampton to decentralize planning to each of the state's seven regional associations of governments. The pilot project allowed the state council to review local plans and to advise the governor on the distribution of MDTA and EOA dollars. Most of the funds were allotted to the seven associations of governments to spend locally according to their plans. Statewide contracts during fiscal year 1974 covered employment service offices, training allowances, services to clients of local manpower programs, and classroom training. In addition, the state created an Office of Veterans Affairs, two positions for minority ombudsmen, and a Public Service Careers program. The WIN program and the JOBS program are sponsored by the State Manpower Planning Council but are funded separately from the comprehensive program grant. South Carolina's pilot comprehensive plan was a similar confederation of ten area boards.

Under CETA, states may promote statewide plans like the Utah and South Carolina regional plans covering the entire state, but most will assume prime sponsorship only for areas not eligible to become independent prime sponsors (cities or counties with less than 100,000 population or those who do not opt to sponsor programs). In any event, the law mandates states to coordinate all manpower-related state agencies, to assist local planners, and to design an overall state plan for sharing resources and reducing duplications of services. States must form state manpower services councils—representing local sponsors, state agencies, organized labor, business, and community groups—to review the plans submitted by localities and state agencies. These councils will also monitor program operations and make an annual report to the governor. Proposed provisions making states the single prime sponsor of manpower programs and giving states power to force state agencies and local sponsors to coordinate their programs were rejected by Congress in 1970. CETA offers the governors an opportunity, and some money if they choose to use it, to coordinate state agencies and local sponsor plans.

Rounding out the CAMPS structure, the 1971 reorganization called for local manpower area planning councils responsible for local manpower plans. The role of elected mayors in the 131 local planning councils paralleled that of governors in the state councils. Often the mayors themselves chaired the councils, and in most cases the council staff worked as part of a mayor's executive office. Moving the planning councils and their staffs into the mayor's office also had its disadvantages. For example, when a new administration took office in Cleveland in 1972, the experienced CAMPS personnel left, leaving the new mayor to form a council, hire staff, and prepare a new annual plan—all in a few months.

Like governors, the mayors were required to balance the membership of councils with client, business, and labor representatives. This usually was accomplished by adding some new faces to the old CAMPS committee. As was true at the state level, representatives from local manpower agencies continued to predominate, and the client group representatives were frequently minority group members who were rarely, if ever, manpower program enrollees. The Boston council, however, was more sensitive to client representation and allowed enrollees in each of the city's three largest programs to choose a council representative. Once encouraged to become active, client spokesmen won two additional seats for a Chinese and a Spanish-speaking representative. From the beginning, federal policymakers gave the metropolitan area virtual planning independence from the state. Local plans were submitted simultaneously to the states and the Department of Labor's regional offices, in effect giving the state bodies little say in the plans. Moreover, local planners were able to direct their comments on comprehensive state plans to the regional offices, leaving any conflicts to be resolved by regional officials rather than by state and local planners.

Some governors protested that under CAMPS the federal government extended power over federal funds to local officials at the expense of gubernatorial authority. The feds justified this action on the ground that the greatest need for coordination was at the local level and that the planning grants might help localities to achieve program efficiency. CETA's call for the formation of state manpower services councils opens the door for states to tackle the problems of coordinating manpower services. While it is unlikely that many governors will want to meddle in the affairs of their large cities, they are obliged to provide local governments with technical assistance if they request it.

The Planning Process

The lead item of most state and local plans was a policy statement by the mayor or governor citing goals for the coming year. Of course, elected officials are sensitive to their local political climate, and they tended to adopt broad policy statements which were not likely to offend any faction. A large part of these plans was a statistical display of the demography, the labor market, and the occupational and industrial characteristics of an area. These data served as a backdrop for estimates of the "universe of need" for manpower services and for projections for expanding and contracting segments of the economy.

In setting forth detailed descriptions of the labor market, plans often failed to determine the supply of job openings "accessible" to the enrollees in manpower programs who were largely a poor, unskilled, or minority clientele.[23] This was a serious lapse in manpower planning since the work experience of clients was limited to secondary labor markets where low wages, unstable employment, and little opportunity for advancement were the rule. This is not to say that it ever was, or will be, easy for manpower planners to locate the desirable, primary labor market jobs, which might provide genuine opportunities for manpower enrollees, and to sort out the dead-end positions from those with promotion possibilities. Local councils normally divided their planning duties among subcommittees. Typical functional subcommittees were concerned with the development of labor market and economic data, program evaluation, and the preparation of the annual plan. Other councils provided for separate subcommittees for client groups or individual programs. Boston's planning council, for example, formed special subcommittees to consider programs for youth and Spanish-speaking citizens and planned another for offenders. A separate subcommittee on planning kept the full council apprised on the secretariat's progress in the actual drafting of the CAMPS plan.

In some instances, the subcommittee arrangement allowed local councils to absorb related manpower functions. Councils often used a subcommittee to serve as the labor market advisory council for the WIN program. These advisory councils were mandated under the 1971 amendments to the Social Security Act which provided that councils would seat representatives of labor, business, and public service employers. Because the WIN advisory council's duties and membership requirements so closely paralleled those of the manpower planning councils, most manpower councils have done double duty, thus satisfying the legislative requirements of WIN.

Data Problems

Although the federal overseers realized the need for sophisticated data to help state and local planning, they settled for easily collected and available information. CAMPS committees often were solely dependent on their local employment service for information on the potential demand for manpower programs. Other data collected by employment service researchers, and which might have been useful to the planners, were not available to them. These data included information about employers from unemployment insurance tax records and samples of employment, hours, occupational distribution, separations, and hires. The employment services supply these data directly to federal agencies, and administrative agreements bar their distribution except in aggregate form. However, a few metropolitan areas received federal support for industry-occupation matrices, job order, and labor turnover statistics. An examination of local plans indicates that manpower planners have taken only limited initiatives to tap the sources available to them from school censuses, welfare case records, city planning commission reports, and information assembled by local business organizations.

To enrich the data base available to local planners, the Bureau of the Census and the Manpower Administration adapted 1970 decennial data for local areas. The added data were only of limited help. Decennial data become stale rather quickly in areas experiencing substantial in- or out-migration. Also, the census tabulations did not always provide the information sought by manpower analysts. For example, the summaries presented the proportions of black men who did not finish high school and who were without jobs, but not the number of blacks unemployed with less than a high school education, and these often were prime candidates for manpower programs.

The need for more accurate data on unemployment, underemployment, and labor demand in states, localities, and poverty areas was recognized in the 1973 manpower law, and CETA mandates the Secretary of Labor to develop reliable methods to measure local labor force data. The motivation was to ensure that CETA funds are distributed according to the formula prescribed by law. The alternative was to use the employment service estimates of labor force data that build on updating census data. It is apparent that Congress felt that the methodology could be improved.

Formulating Recommendations

Even the limited planning capability of state and local CAMPS committees was hardpressed by the constraint to await the annual pronouncement of federal guidelines before fashioning their plans to suit the federal requirements. Although planning presumably was a year-round function for the manpower planning councils—research, evaluation, and the development of alternative strategies—councils actually had little motivation to perform these functions. First, federal requirements left little room for them to apply their findings to the distribution of funds. Second, the due date for the plans often left little time for preparation. Only after federal directives were issued, including the next year's budget allotments, did planning move into high gear. Program sponsors rarely did any serious work until after the money was on the table. CAMPS remained, therefore, an annual paper exercise performed for federal officials, and true planning was held in check by adherence to federal directives.

The rhetoric of the 1971 revisions promised local councils a greater influence on budget allocations. Planners were asked to set out how current efforts met the needs they had identified and to measure the effectiveness and efficiency of current program operations. The realities, of course, did not live up to the rhetoric. What was intended to be the heart of the manpower plans, the assessment of current programs and recommendations for the next year's funding, demonstrated how much of a perfunctory exercise the councils' actions really were. The local councils received a list of programs and their assigned budget allocations from a Department of Labor regional office, which placed severe limits on any changes they might want to recommend. The acceptance of a local or state plan and its recommendations by the regional office, moreover, was not a legally binding guarantee of funding. Therefore, local program sponsors continued to negotiate separately with federal regional representatives for their annual allotment of funds under various manpower authorizations. And since there was no prospect of those committees effecting a change in resource allocation among programs, they had little reason to make more than a cursory examination of the programs' impact on their communities.

Evaluation

Local council members questioned the value of program evaluation, since they could not affect program funding, but federal officials continued to tempt them to believe that they eventually would get control of manpower funds. Responding to federal inducements, some local councils turned to the federally designed manpower information systems for the basic data needed for program performance evaluation. The scrutiny of these data led to a new round of criticism to the effect that data collection often was spotty and inadequate to meet evaluation needs and that some program administrators withheld much of the data that they had collected. To improve data disclosure, a Labor Department directive required regional offices, state agencies, and program operators to provide, upon request of local councils, reports on enrollees, costs, and program activities. Internal operations and management reports, "sensitive" material, intra-agency memoranda, were outside the scope of the directive. Although this was an important breakthrough for planners, some of whom had been unaware of the data that existed, bureaucratic penchant for secrecy and control over data was not to be changed by a single directive. The evaluators continued to complain that program agents were withholding information or only grudgingly yielding it.

Of course, receiving and assembling the data is only the first hurdle. The development of evaluation techniques for social programs remains a thorny problem; improved data alone will not resolve controversies concerning goals that are implicit in the evaluation of these programs. The Cleveland manpower council, for example, determined that for fiscal 1974 its evaluation committee would report on program efficiency. But Cleveland evaluators found that the appropriate criteria were not easy to define. If efficiency was defined simply as keeping costs per successful placement low, Cleveland planners would, in effect, be encouraging program administrators to enroll the most job-ready clients. Another problem they faced was how to make the punishment fit the crime. If a critical evaluation was translated into a reduction of funds for a poorly administered program, the clients served by the program would be punished for inept management.

The Planning Area

Manpower planning at the local level is determined within labor markets. The USES designates 150 areas as major labor markets, which generally coincide with the Standard Metropolitan Statistical Areas. However, CETA designates some 500 prime sponsors whose boundaries are political.

Traditional definitions of the labor market include one or more central cities and the surrounding geographic area in which employers and workers are able to exchange job offers and labor services. But not all labor market analysts consider this definition workable. They have gathered persuasive evidence that job markets vary among workers by occupation, sex, age, and socioeconomic characteristics and that workers' mobility in any labor market can be hindered by personal, social, and institutional barriers.

Any metropolitan or statewide planning area is likely to have a variety of these labor markets within its scope, which complicates the task of the planning body. The existence of political boundaries are likely to present further problems. For example, most manpower delivery systems are centered in the cities. Dividing the manpower pie among all jurisdictions of over 100,000 population, as CETA does, will mean many areas will see a redistribution of funds favoring suburban towns and counties, which could fragment real labor market planning.

The Boston area provides a good example of the difficulties in reconciling manpower planning to an area of workable size. As in most metropolitan areas, blue-collar job opportunities that could be filled by Boston residents are expanding in the suburbs and declining in the city, while technical and professional employees live in the suburbs and commute to city jobs. Before 1972, the Boston CAMPS attempted to cover the entire Boston major labor market area and, coincidentally, the SMSA, which stretches for thirty miles around Boston and encompasses five counties and some eighty small towns and cities.[24] Because of the multiple jurisdictions, a fully representative council for the labor market area was unworkable. In 1972, Boston planners accepted the suggestion of the state office of manpower affairs that the council cover only Suffolk County, in which Boston is located, and the city of Brookline in neighboring Norfolk County. As a result, planning continued to focus largely on the city. Under CETA, the Boston planning council will represent only the city of Boston, and another city in the SMSA, Cambridge, has also been designated as a prime sponsor. The smaller jurisdictions in the Boston area were given the choice of entering into a multijurisdictional arrangement with either of the two designated prime sponsors or of leaving the responsibility for their manpower services to the governor.

In other areas, like Cleveland, the centrifugal force opposing multi-jurisdiction, or labor market, planning was largely owing to political differences between the city and neighboring areas. Cleveland is located in Cuyahoga County, and the SMSA includes Geauga, Lake, and Medina Counties. The original Cleveland CAMPS was city-oriented, but under the 1971 revisions the state council selected this body to represent all of Cuyahoga, Geauga, and Lake Counties. Even then the Cleveland manpower council focused its attention on the city's manpower problems and programs, while laying some ground-work for the requirement that fiscal 1974 plans or CETA plans would require the approval of elected officials in jurisdictions over 100,000 eligible to be independent prime sponsors. In the Cleveland area, Cuyahoga and Lake Counties, plus the city of Parma (also in Cuyahoga County) met CETA's prime sponsorship criteria.

During 1973 the Cleveland planning council expanded its membership to include representatives of the area's county commissions and some suburbs, but the fiscal 1974 plan still did not reflect the change in any redistribution of funds to the other areas. It is little wonder, then, that the four jurisdictions outside of Cleveland eligible for manpower funds under CETA balked at the first efforts of city planners to create a consortium. However, in the end, the Cleveland planning council was able to overcome political differences and negotiate an areawide manpower consortium, which has delegated administrative authority to the city. Beginning in fiscal 1975, the Cleveland area will be experimenting with metropolitan planning and program operation.

There are other areas in which multijurisdictional planning or the joint operation of manpower programs may have grown strong enough in the last few years to offset political centrifugal pressures. Milwaukee offers an unusual example of a solution to city-county problems. When the Milwaukee CAMPS was reconstituted as a manpower area planning council in 1972, the city's mayor, Henry Maier, deferred to the county executive as the prime sponsor. Mayor Maier's action was based on his ten years of frustration with federal social programs and on his judgment that the city would still get a fair share of manpower monies. His attitude toward the planning council has been cooperative, and the council respects the mayor's prerogatives and has sought and received his advice before formally submitting its plan. This accommodation reflects the fact that there is little conflict of interest between the city and its suburban neighbors over manpower programs. On one hand, the suburbs have little need, and they care less about manpower programs which focus on the needs of the disadvantaged. On the other hand, the city is satisfied to divest itself of planning responsibilities.

The county executive, John Doyne, represents eighteen primarily white suburban juridictions in addition to the city and was only barely acquainted with manpower when he assumed the duties of planning chairman. His manpower experience was limited to associations with the county's welfare department through WIN and a county-funded work and training program for welfare recipients. Doyne has not faced unusual political problems within the suburban area or on the planning council. The Intergovernmental Cooperation Council, composed of representatives of eighteeen suburban jurisdictions, has been invited to send a representative to meetings, but one rarely comes. The sentiment throughout the suburbs is indifferent rather than hostile since they feel manpower programs will not benefit their neighborhoods. None of the spokesmen for suburban jurisdictions were interested, for example, in public service careers funds.

Although Milwaukee's labor market area as defined by the SMSA includes three neighboring counties, Washington, Ozaukee, and Waukesha, Milwaukee County has not been overanxious to draw them into a multijurisdictional arrangement for manpower funding. The three counties do not share Milwaukee's inner city problems and are reluctant to become dominated by Milwaukee's political clout or social needs. Instead, before CETA, they chose to join as an area manpower planning board under state auspices and now have organized a joint area manpower planning council on a tri-county basis. Though the Milwaukee planning council would like to have a formal multijurisdictional arrangement with the other counties, if only for the increased funding this would bring, the council is willing to wait for such an arrangement and is not trying to force the other counties to agree to a coalition with which they might become dissatisfied.

A highly touted model for multijurisdictional manpower planning has been metropolitan government: a combination of city and suburbs. In Miami/Dade County, Florida, for example, manpower programs for the city/county area are planned and operated centrally through the executive office of the county manager. However, the effectiveness of its metropolitan government format has been credited in large part to the socioeconomic similarities of the city and county and the weakness of established political, labor, and ethnic organizations.[25] Nationwide there is not always such a favorable environment for metropolitan cooperation.

Another possibility is a metropolitan Council of Governments, a confederation where normally each jurisdiction has one vote and where each represents another government, not a voting constituency. In most COGs, central cities do not have a vote proportional to their size or to the extent of their problems. As a result, the needs of minorities and the disadvantaged often are underrepresented.[26] The most far-reaching example of the use of a COG for manpower planning is the Metropolitan Kansas City Planning Area, which covers three major cities, 103 smaller cities, and eight counties in two states. There, the Mid-America Regional Council, as the COG is called, established a manpower planning department by consolidating planning grants which had been made separately to the mayors of Kansas City, Kansas, and Kansas City and Independence, Missouri, as a supplement to its other regional planning activities. Five local planning boards—one for each city, one for the Kansas counties, and one for the Missouri counties—determine local needs, and a twenty-seven-member metropolitan manpower planning board oversees the areawide plan. The metro board membership is weighted in favor of the two largest cities, each having nine representatives, while Independence and the counties each have one representative. Although much effort has gone into organizing this unique planning arrangement, Mid-America planners remained under the same planning constraints as their brethren elsewhere, and there were few noticeable changes in the planning recommendations for the area during 1973.

With CETA's provision for a bonus of up to 10 percent for multi-jurisdictional plans which cover a substantial portion of the labor market area, the potential for more intergovernmental combinations has increased. Counties have been given real bargaining power—additional money during years of retrenched budgets—if they choose to negotiate with adjoining cities or other counties. However, rather than undertaking negotiations with other communities, many newly endowed sponsors may choose to adopt a wait-and-see attitude. Past intergovernmental relations, good and bad, also will affect the shaping multijurisdictional arrangements.

The Players

Given the range of experiences states and localities have had in the manpower arena, another question arises about the selection of groups to be represented in manpower planning. CETA's requirements cover the waterfront: specifically, client and community-based organizations, the employment service, education and training agencies and institutions, business, labor, and, where appropriate, agriculture.

The value of linking the manpower service system to the employment service, the oldest and largest manpower agency, needs no elaboration. Other agencies that are part of the human resources establishment—public education, vocational education and rehabilitation programs—

have played at best a passive role in shaping past manpower policies. But as long as these agencies receive federal funds for skill training and special education programs, their efforts are important supplements to the efforts of a manpower sponsor.

In the private sector, employers' organizations, labor unions, and the representatives of program participants all have a vested interest in manpower planning. In several instances, employer groups have stimulated significant changes in manpower planning. In Cleveland, early attempts to coordinate manpower programs were started by the Metropolitan Cleveland Jobs Council, an employer-dominated group. In Baltimore, the business community urged the mayor to investigate the feasibility of a computerized job order system to reduce duplicative job development activity, and thus stimulated the development of the job bank. A larger effort, the National Alliance of Businessmen, created in 1968, brought many local employers into the manpower system for the first time by charging them with the responsibility of hiring and training the disadvantaged. Labor unions have a special interest in federally sponsored outreach programs to boost minority union membership and share with employers the responsibility for hiring graduates of manpower skill training programs. In sum, good relations with those who control job opportunities are essential for the manpower sponsor.

Obtaining participation of representatives of the poor, disadvantaged, and minorities has been a longstanding problem for manpower planners; often this representation has come through the community action agencies (CAAs), established under the Economic Opportunity Act of 1964. The goal of including manpower clients in planning has been written into the new law, and past acceptance of minority representatives in manpower planning has been encouraging. A 1970 study on the activities of CAMPS committees in 133 areas found that the CAAs were at least formally represented on each. Furthermore, the relationship between mayors and the CAAs was in most cases found to be encouraging.[27] Nonetheless, there are few areas where former manpower enrollees help to do manpower planning.

In Albuquerque the city Office of Manpower Programs has perhaps gone farther than most cities in assuring the antipoverty agency a continuing role in manpower planning. A formal agreement between the city and the CAA guarantees that a third of the membership of the planning council is nominated by the CAA; that neighborhood hearings are held in which community spokesmen could discuss the plan; and, more important, that the CAA has been funded to provide independent evaluations of the city's manpower efforts.

Linking Planning and Delivery

How to join manpower planners and deliverers of manpower services is another unresolved issue. Although CETA vests responsibility with the chief elected official for establishing his advisory planning council and for administering the programs, it is likely that there will actually be a variety of subcontractors who will actually deliver manpower services. And as was learned from earlier experiences, multiple contractors, even when they share office space or a boss, do not necessarily have effective planning and operational links.

But a linkage is crucial if planning is not to occur in a vacuum. Planners must have the backing not only to allocate and reallocate the funds but also to exercise the authority to terminate contracts. They must have an adequate staff to monitor the programs and collect information necessary to choose among available manpower strategies. Unless the deliverers of services are accountable to the planners and decisionmakers, decentralization will have failed in its goal of making the operation of manpower programs responsive to local needs.

Although a single prime sponsor having both planning and operation responsibilities might make this accountability more direct, the advantages of allowing more than one prime sponsor to vie for manpower contracts cannot be ignored. Different manpower agencies have demonstrated that they can better service special clients. Moreover competition among sponsors can encourage economically efficient resource allocation.

Weighing the CAMPS Experience

Like many federal efforts, CAMPS was announced with much optimistic rhetoric, exalting the promise of coordination among federal agencies at all levels of government. CAMPS committees gave agency representatives a chance to sit down together and find out what others were doing, but offered little incentive to participating organizations to change what they were doing, even if a CAMPS meeting might have disclosed that change was desirable. Where attempts were made to use the planning process to effect changes, much of the dynamics of backroom sessions was not apparent in the written plan.

Local planners were confronted annually with a federal budget and a set of federal programs. They had to assemble meaningful data on local clients and the local labor market and catalog the frequently overlapping programs of the local delivery agents. Mixing all of these variables together with a dash of politics, supplied by the responsible elected official, they were expected to generate a plan for the next year's manpower services.

However, by viewing the problems through the "categorical microscope," designers of federal programs left local planners no choice but to accept an array of programs often offering overlapping services. Outreach, intake, testing, counseling, job development, placement, follow-up, as well as such supportive services as health care, transportation assistance, and child care were common to many manpower programs. The fragmented delivery of these services at the local level was a roadblock to a comprehensive manpower plan.

Moreover, plans were made with a lingering uncertainty about whether federal officials would use them. The limited ability of planning councils to influence the actions of federal administrators is illustrated by the fate of the Milwaukee Job Corps. In 1970 federal officials solicited suggestions for an all-male residential center in the Milwaukee area. No agreement on a site had been reached two years later when the national office unilaterally selected a contractor and signed a lease for the center. Members of both the state and local planning councils complained to national and regional Job Corps officials about the selection of the site and the contractor without the benefit of state and local advice. The state was willing to amend its plan to include the Job Corps site, but the local council refused to endorse the Job Corps plan without consultation. This exercise of muscle by the Milwaukee planning council cost the community its Job Corps. The national office chose not to renegotiate, and thereby risk wasting funds in a delay, and took its money elsewhere.

The CAMPS guidelines for fiscal year 1972 signaled a shift in federal policy. The revision failed, however, to address the most significant limitation of CAMPS as a planning system. First, the CAMPS mechanism was superimposed on the planning that sponsors did in the course of regular program operations. Even the requirement that councils evaluate the efforts of sponsors did little to increase the councils' impact, although the exercise did familiarize them with labor market and program data. The mandates to evaluate and recommend did not include the powers to reallocate funds or to modify program operations. To program sponsors, the evaluations that counted, in terms of next year's funds, were those of federal officials.

The guidelines for fiscal 1972 were not without impact. Possibly the most significant change was the requirement that governors and mayors assume responsibility for their manpower planning councils, and in almost every case they responded. The elected officials convened the councils, moved the federally funded support staff into their offices, and in many cases took an active interest in their area's manpower operations. The evolution of the involvement of state and local officials and the development of staff capabilities in their jurisdictions are perhaps the most important contributions of CAMPS in light of CETA.

As an experiment in social policy, CAMPS offers few examples of locally conceived innovations in manpower programming. The guidelines instructed planners to stay out of program operation and administration, hampering attempts by planners to get a real feel for manpower problems. Several cities and states went beyond the intent of CAMPS and established human resources departments to consolidate the delivery of an entire range of human resources services. The federally sponsored planning system contributed the initial impetus to the establishment of the new departments, but the system offered little incentive for the action.

CAMPS did not provide an adequate machinery to cope with the difficulties of planning for a labor market area. No federal directive will be able to resolve the intergovernmental conflicts of states and jurisdictions within states or of the variety of jurisdictions in any major metropolitan area. In the CAMPS records, there were few examples of successful multijurisdictional arrangements. Whether the carrot of a 10 percent increase in funding included in the 1973 law will bring planning areas closer to the labor marketwide goal is uncertain.

Over the past three years, the CAMPS guidelines dangled the tempting prospect of local control before the planning councils and the elected officials. Even if the promises went unfulfilled as the debate over legislation became protracted, the directives raised the potentials of manpower reform. The responses of governors, mayors, county officials, public interest groups, Congress, program sponsors, and independent evaluators to the policy pronouncements of CAMPS directives were no doubt instrumental in gaining support for CETA.

The Lessons of Fiscal 1974

Even before CETA became law, federal officials offered states and localities a limited opportunity to plan the allocation of funds for manpower programs. If the ways in which cities responded to the opportunity to set priorities and distribute dollars among sponsors is indicative of the way the councils will plan under CETA, changes can be expected to evolve only gradually. In many cases, planning councils made no substantial reallocations. Decisions to expand programs naturally were much easier to make than recommendations to reduce a sponsor's allocation. Where councils chose to recommend major budget cuts or the elimination of particular programs, the constituencies of the programs often found a means to get their piece of the action reinstated in the final plan.

The councils' freedom to make changes during fiscal 1974 planning was limited by two significant constraints. First, the federal manpower budget for fiscal 1974 was retrenched drastically. Normal difficulties in planning were compounded by announcements that funds would be impounded; but the magnitude of the cuts was not made public for some time. The cuts were distributed unevenly, and they followed reductions earlier in 1973 in the budgets of ongoing programs. Thus, much of the planning councils' time had to be spent in developing salable budget reductions. The second important restriction on planning was the requirement that only sponsors who had received fiscal year 1973 funds were eligible for 1974 monies. Fewer dollars and the eligibility proscriptions on new sponsors limited innovative manpower efforts, assuming the planners would have ventured to initiate new programs or reorganizations if they had the resources and freedom to act.

Not all local planning councils were well prepared for their new responsibilities to allocate funds according to their own priorities. Milwaukee's experience may have been typical. The secretariat head of its planning council was appointed late in 1972, and invitations for membership to meet the requirements of the revised CAMPS guidelines were further delayed. With the fiscal year 1974 plan due in April 1973, the newly formed council decided to treat its first plan as a learning experience for an inexperienced staff and council.

Milwaukee's hesitation in its first planning year indicates that planning councils that must be built from scratch, or those with many new members, will need a start-up period before any planning sophistication can be expected. The Milwaukee planning staff spent much of its time during the last two months of 1972 learning about manpower planning. At council meetings, the newly selected members representing the private and nonprofit agencies and client groups had to learn their manpower ABC's before substantive deliberations could be initiated. It is not unreasonable to expect a similar lag in other areas or perhaps an even longer one in counties that have not had the benefit of previous manpower program experience.

Manpower planning councils that ventured to propose reallocations in their manpower budgets found that the countervailing power of the threatened interest groups often could offset the councils' best laid plans. In July 1973, when the Cleveland planning council was notified of an additional 5 percent reduction in the city's 1974 manpower budget, the decision of whose ox to gore set off a struggle in the manpower community. The evaluation committee recommended that Cleveland's MDTA-institutional, the three NYC programs, and the "hometown plan" bear the brunt of the reduction. In a packed house, representatives of the Cleveland Board of Education and Ohio Bureau of Employment Services pleaded their case and succeeded in convincing the evaluation committee that it had misjudged the effectiveness of the training program. In the end, MDTA-institutional funds were partially reinstated, and the manager of the city's MDTA Skills Center was left to pass around the necessary reductions. Much of the success of the school board and the employment service in fighting off the budget cut was no doubt owing to their political power in the manpower community and their desire to protect their slice of the manpower pie. The city human resources agency did not wage such a battle on behalf of NYC, which had received a scathing federal evaluation, and the "hometown plan" sponsor was not as successful in its own cause.

Albuquerque planners encountered a somewhat different problem in trying to eliminate Project SER and the Opportunities Industrialization

Center from the fiscal 1974 budget. The planning council's task force on adult training felt that SER's services—direct placement, job development, basic education, high school equivalency training, and clerical skills training—although targeted for Chicanos, closely paralleled services available from the local MDTA Skills Center. Therefore, it was argued, costs could be reduced if SER's clients were served by the Skills Center. The task force had the choice of bowing to SER's political clout and presumed record for good performance or of living up to the goals of comprehensive manpower planning by eliminating a duplicative agency. They heroically chose the latter route. OIC, which provided services similar to those of SER, but for blacks, was scheduled for cutback because its costs per placement were found to be too high.

The elimination of SER and OIC survived a public meeting where the planning council presented its recommendations. However, since the plan had to be approved by the city and county commissioners, SER and OIC used the intervening time to lobby for restoration of their funds. The final budget approval by the city commission was delayed until the Albuquerque Office of Manpower Programs and SER negotiated a reorganization of the program that would allow its continuation. The negotiators decided that SER's budget would actually be raised and its staff size maintained. OIC took its case before the county commission, which offered the Office of Manpower Programs a $30,000 grant to put OIC back in the budget. In the final agreement, OIC's funding was restored out of the federal pocketbook, and the county funds were put to other uses. Albuquerque's comprehensive manpower concept had taken a back seat to political peace owing to the success of the minority organizations' argument that competition among categorical programs would improve the system's ability to serve different groups of clients.

Boston offers another example of a 1974 plan that attempted to capitalize on the comparative advantages of existing sponsors in its effort to confront the problem of a substantially smaller manpower budget. The experience of Boston's community action agency (ABCD) with youth programs preceded the passage of OEO legislation, and ABCD was directed to create a youth employment and training center based on its NYC Out-of-School program. The Adult Work Crew for chronic unemployables, which mainly had been serving alcoholics, was to operate a readjustment center for ex-offenders, one of the new locally determined target groups. OIC's institutional training for black adults was expanded with the addition of an MDTA course, while ABCD's skill training courses for adults and its New Careers program were trimmed. Courses in English as a second language were funded under the auspices of Chinese and Spanish-speaking community organizations. A Spanish-speaking community agency received monies for a neighborhood employment center. As in the past, ABCD was to specialize in work experience programs and in services to the most disadvantaged groups, now identified as youth and ex-offenders. However, ABCD also was expected to bear a considerable portion of the budget retrenchment—its New Careers funds were halved, adult skill training was cut back, and two of its twelve neighborhood centers were eliminated—and ABCD challenged the planning council's authority for these cutbacks in court. CETA should put to rest such challenges in the future.

ABCD was not alone in absorbing the impact of the budget cuts. Three relatively expensive MDTA paramedical courses were dropped. The Boston School Department, the MDTA-institutional sponsor, had its programs for adult basic communication, English as a second language, and skill training reduced to accommodate the smaller budget, and the council recommended no increase in the size of the MDTA skills center. But the Boston School Department protested to the planning council and, despite questions about the record of the skills center to sustain its capacity enrollment in the past, additional funds were found for it.

In this first glance at decentralized planning, it appears that local planners have not strayed too far from the existing pattern of programs and sponsors. In some areas, the recognition of the need to satisfy community-based ethnic groups and powerful manpower agencies may only perpetuate what one observer termed a "new parochialism" in manpower programs. Further, many areas have chosen to continue to distribute manpower funds by function, much as they previously were allocated by the federal decisionmakers. Perhaps the somewhat random method of the feds was not so far out of line with local desires as some have asserted.

CETA mandates the administration of manpower programs by elected officials and encourages multijurisdictional arrangements.

Local decisions on the allocation of funds among subcontractors and services will be made on the basis of recommendations by the planning councils. By giving the state and local officials budget authority, congressional and administration policymakers have expressed confidence that evaluation and decisionmaking at state and local levels can become an effective and efficient process, not just an annual ritual performed for federal overseers.

Chapter 4

Comprehensive Programs:
New Systems to Repair the Old

A primary aim of planning was the identification and development of linkages among agencies and institutions involved in manpower efforts. Before the passage of CETA, manpower planning councils had limited authority to reshape the way manpower funds were used at the community level and could do very little to eliminate the number of overlapping manpower programs in their communities. The best that the planning councils could do was to exhort team play in the manpower arena. Since Labor Department officials predominated and funded state and local efforts, appeals for cooperation were taken by other agencies to mean "you coo; we operate."

The key word in the promotion of manpower planning as a solution to the problems of the manpower system was coordination. At the same time, the federal government was proposing an alternative solution to the fragmented state of manpower organization—so-called comprehensive programs—whose goal was to provide funds to a single sponsor to purchase or deliver a wide range of services for selected clientele. The assumption was that coordination could be acheived within the single institution as it collected the area's manpower services under its umbrella. The experience of local institutions with comprehensive programs is a significant precedent for the decentralization and decategorization strategies advanced by the 1973 manpower law, which has authorized planners to design their own versions of comprehensive manpower services.

Community-Based Antipoverty Programs

A central goal of the War on Poverty was the design of a strategy to create comprehensive programs at the neighborhood level. The antipoverty policymakers believed the best way to address local problems was to ensure that residents of the communities had a significant role in shaping services to fit their needs. The grand design envisioned in antipoverty rhetoric was to fund community institutions in neighborhoods where the greatest need for social programs existed.

These institutions also became a base from which those affected by the programs could influence administrators and bureaucrats to better serve the poor. Manpower was to be only one part of the concerted onslaught on poverty; however, antipoverty funds were too limited to implement the comprehensive approach on a broad scale.

The Community Action Agencies

The antipoverty Community Action Program (CAP) resulted in the establishment of over 1000 CAAs in its first two years. But lacking resources to provide a single comprehensive social program to aid the poor, CAAs became pilot catchalls for nearly every type of antipoverty effort: education, manpower, health, legal aid, and social services. Most OEO manpower funds originated from federal contracts to run the "national emphasis" programs, which included the Neighborhood Youth Corps, Operation Mainstream, Public Service Careers, and the Concentrated Employment Program. In spite of the fact that the administration of these programs was eventually transferred from the Office of Economic Opportunity to the Department of Labor, CAAs continued to sponsor them. National funds also were available for legal services, a variety of programs for migrant workers, and Head Start projects to provide education to preschoolers.

To fulfill their goals of programs structured to fit local needs, CAAs developed different strategies. Many made their greatest impact by changing local institutions through community organization and mobilization.[28] In some areas, community action zeroed in on traditional institutions supplying manpower services—the local employment service and school system. In other cities, manpower projects took a back seat to other CAA activities such as child care, health care, and legal aid or other social services. Whatever their specialty, many CAAs found their position as advocates for the poor and minorities conflicted with the ideals of cooperation among existing social service agencies. In general, CAAs offered comprehensive programs to the extent that they were able to collect a variety of new federal contracts.

Boston's antipoverty agency, ABCD, chose to provide manpower programs both with local initiative money and through federal contracts for Neighborhood Youth Corps, Concentrated Employment Program, Operation Mainstream, and New Careers. Beginning in

1966, ABCD began to establish neighborhood employment centers and, with the addition of the federal training and work experience programs, the centers were the bases from which the agency could recruit neighborhood residents, place them in a program, and later in a job. Eventually, three orientation centers and thirteen neighborhood centers were created. In the rhetoric of the era, the centers were the key element in a "comprehensive program of manpower and employment services" for Boston's poor.

By 1971, a third of the agency's budget went into manpower efforts. One explanation for this emphasis may be that an early ABCD executive director previously headed manpower programs in New Haven, Connecticut, before coming to Boston in 1966 and was especially sensitive to manpower issues. But the main reason ABCD became heavily involved in manpower was that its leaders believed that the local employment service, the school system, and the vocational education establishment had failed to serve inner city residents. ABCD began as a catalyst, hoping to stimulate traditional agencies to take steps to serve poor inner city residents. However, OEO funding enabled the antipoverty agency to operate its own manpower programs, as researchers Morris A. Horowitz and Irwin L. Herrnstadt described it, stepping on the toes of the established agencies as it moved into jurisdictions which they claimed, but did not occupy.

Nevertheless, ABCD and the Boston employment service were able to establish a working relationship under which employment service staff worked in the neighborhood centers. Despite occasional clashes over a proper manpower role for each agency and the resentment felt by the employment service and the school system, ABCD was able to carve out a primary role in Boston manpower with the aid of federal funds. After fiscal 1972, however, its antipoverty programs began to get less of the city's manpower budget, as the WIN program and the PEP received priority attention.

A continuing controversy on which antipoverty warriors focused was the relative emphasis that was to be expended on planning and action programs. Originally, the antipoverty strategists intended to require the CAAs to develop and submit formal plans as a funding prerequisite, but an amendment in the House of Representatives deleted planning from the 1964 law. Three years later, after the Bureau of the Budget raised the question of plans with OEO, Congress added amendments to the Economic Opportunity Act which explicitly required that the CAAs "adopt a systematic approach" to the planning and implementation of their programs.[29] Congress ignored, however, the fact that few of the funded projects could venture beyond the experimental pilot stage.

Unlike the CAMPS program under which the Labor Department eventually provided separate funds for planning staffs, the CAA planning monies were part of their basic grants. OEO offered additional support in the form of meager technical assistance and training in the grant process and made trained VISTA volunteers available. OEO chose not to implement the 1967 amendment and require the CAAs to submit plans in a predetermined CAMPS-like format, Instead, the agencies were instructed to reflect their long-run and short-run plans in their grant applications.

Proposed budget cuts and the end of a separate antipoverty agency cannot undo several of the contributions of community action agencies. One of these has been their role in moving neighborhood leaders into better positions, both in the CAAs and in other community agencies, and serving as a stepping stone to better positions in the private sector. In many communities, CAA spokesmen have become recognized representatives of the poor and minorities and have been asked to sit on manpower planning councils. As these councils undertake control of the local manpower budget under CETA, this role of maintaining a voice for the poor in manpower affairs will become even more important.

Model Cities

The Model Cities program, initiated by the Demonstration Cities and Metropolitan Development Act of 1966, was more planning oriented than the Community Action Program, but both measures shared the philosophy that city poverty problems could best be attacked with comprehensive programs that enjoyed the support and input of local citizens. The 1966 law sought to combine physical urban renewal with other social efforts—education, health, crime reduction, manpower, and economic development—in order to improve all aspects of the slum environment. In contrast to the CAAs, city demonstration agencies (CDAs), which were funded by the Department of Housing and Urban Development (HUD), were publicly sponsored and placed under the direction of elected officials. Where plans had taken a back seat to action in most CAAs, the CDAs were to prepare and submit for HUD approval detailed five-year plans in advance of implementing their strategies. The HUD-funded planning grants, which totaled $22.2 million for 150 cities by April 1971, covered up to 80 percent of the planning costs in each city. Funds to operate projects were contingent on HUD's acceptance of the city's plan.

Despite the difference in sponsorship, Model Cities projects shared some problems with CAAs. Most significantly, the federal commitment in money and talent was too small for the projects to have a noticeable impact on urban blight even when resources were targeted in small areas of the cities. Moreover, attempts to make services comprehensive forced the sponsors to spread their resources too thinly. The goal of reducing duplications in the area's social services proved elusory.

The architects of the Model Cities legislation intentionally worded the requirement for citizen involvement in vague terms so as to avoid the controversy that occurred when OEO attempted to implement the EOA provision for "maximum feasible participation of the residents of the areas and members of the groups served" (P. L. 88-452, Sec. 211(f) (1)). In the case of Model Cities, no formula existed for assuring neighborhood involvement, but Congress prescribed that membership on community action boards be divided equally among public officials, private groups, and the poor.

Critics charged that the planning requirements, plus the close relationship of Model Cities agencies to city halls, isolated the program from neighborhood influence. Low voter turnouts in neighborhood board elections reinforced this criticism. There were few cases where citizens gained veto power over proposals or where neighborhood representatives had enough control over funds to hire their own planners. The common practice was to have a neighborhood advisory committee without planning funds and to have the residents elect representatives on the policy board.[30] However, citizen participation in publicly sponsored programs requires leadership from elected officials; this was a missing element in many Model Cities programs.

But like the community action program, Model Cities experienced a broad spectrum of interactions between local governments and citizens. Although several of the more militant resident boards received most of the publicity, instance of constructive community efforts outweighed the futile endeavors. After several years, Model Cities experiments contributed to the development of positive attitudes among public officials and their staffs toward citizen participation.[31]

The future of the Model Cities program now depends on the outcome of the Nixon administration proposal to absorb it under the Better Communities Act in 1975, a special revenue sharing proposal to encompass all community development efforts. CETA's tight budget probably will keep many areas from salvaging Model Cities manpower projects to include them in community manpower programs. And, if the Better Communities Act is passed, it is unclear how local governments will divide their funds among Model Cities projects and other urban renewal activities.

Antipoverty Agency Contributions

Organizational and strategy differences notwithstanding, the Model Cities and community action programs overlapped both geographically and functionally. The CAAs generally served larger poverty areas than the targeted Model Cities neighborhoods, and cooperation between the two varied. A list of Model Cities projects closely resembles those of the CAAs—education and day care, health, urban renewal and development, housing, and manpower. Like the CAAs, the comprehensive nature of Model Cities plans depended on federally funded projects, not on coordination with already existing programs. But in contrast to the CAAs, Model Cities agencies were not constrained by prepackaged national programs. Instead, far more time and money was expended in planning for local varieties of five-year Model Cities programs.

Both Model Cities and CAAs were part of a broad shift toward local administration of publicly funded programs during the late 1960s and early 1970s that saw growing minority participation in city health departments, welfare boards, hospitals, United Funds, YMCAs, and related agencies.[32] The membership of professional associations in the field of public administration changed, and minority-oriented public interest groups were formed. In many cities, it was a challenge by the CAAs that pressured the employment service to establish outreach offices in ghetto neighborhoods and encouraged them to hire a minority staff. Community-based expertise is one contribution of the CAAs and Model Cities programs to decentralization, however dispersed its quality or quantity. Beginning in fiscal 1975, the outcome of such investments in local capacity to manage social programs will be tested.

In some areas, the activities undertaken by CAAs and Model Cities agencies have been absorbed by local governments. In the early days of the Community Action Program, the conflicts between city halls and the CAAs were much publicized. In the 1967 "Green Amendment" to the EOA, Congress required that CAAs be brought directly under the sponsorship of the mayor or that they receive his approval to continue to independently sponsor antipoverty programs. Despite the heat generated over the amendment, only a few CAAs went public; most elected officials chose to keep their distance from the controversial CAAs and not to disturb the operations of the ones that had gained community respect. Either way, the CAAs developed a reputation as local lobbyists for the clients of federal social programs.

The contributions of the CAAs and Model Cities agencies to the development of local know-how in the so-called art of federal grantsmanship and the pressure they put on local elected officials to take an interest in federal social programs contrast with their inability to coordinate federal programs and to deliver "comprehensive" services. Their role in manpower planning was defined, on one hand, by their agreement to participate in the CAMPS process and, on the other hand, by legislative mandates that they plan and administer their grants separately. While Congress proclaimed the charge to coordinate, it did not provide sufficient funding of community-based efforts or an effective chain of command for the antipoverty fight.

Comprehensive Work and Training Programs

The futility of establishing comprehensive manpower programs by legislative mandate was apparent in the history of the Comprehensive Work and Training Program. Coordination was central to President Johnson's 1967 manpower message to Congress. An examination of the War on Poverty by the Senate Subcommittee on Employment, Manpower and Poverty, conducted in 1967, found that most CAAs were failing to coordinate local antipoverty efforts. In the case of manpower, Secretary Willard Wirtz pleaded that the Department of Labor should assume leadership through the newly created CAMPS committees and Concentrated Employment Programs.[33] But Senator Joseph Clark of Pennsylvania and his staff favored amending the antipoverty law to provide for a single prime sponsor for all EOA-funded manpower programs in the area except JOBS, in-school work support, and the Job Corps. Although the Senate version explicitly required the CAAs to be the sponsors of CWTPs, the House did not agree, and no presumptive prime sponsors were specified in the law.

Having been mandated once again to coordinate local manpower programs, OEO and the Department of Labor were left to work out the "details," meaning actual implementation. They agreed to reinstate the prime sponsorship role of the CAAs unless compelling program reasons required otherwise. When the July 1968 deadline for compliance with the law was reached, the two agencies quietly abandoned the program and reached an informal agreement that the CEPs fulfilled the congressional intent. Without any further agreement to make the CWTP operational, the program drifted into limbo and the agencies' interest lagged.

However, the concept of single prime sponsorship was never officially shelved; by 1969 Secretary of Labor George P. Shultz reported to the Senate that 177 sites had been definitely selected for CWTPs and 44 others might be added.[34] But the CWTPs only existed on paper, and two years later when the EOA came up for its next reauthorization, the discussion focused on the Nixon administration's manpower revenue sharing bill. The issue was still comprehensive programs, but the focus had changed.

The Concentrated Employment Program

The Johnson administration's interest in a special employment program in ghetto neighborhoods was aroused by Labor Department surveys conducted in 1966 which showed concentrations of unemployment in urban neighborhoods between 6 and 15 percent. Many of the employed in these areas did not earn enough to pull their families out of poverty.[35] Therefore, in March 1967, before Congress had enacted the EOA amendments that authorized "special programs which concentrate work and training resources in urban and rural areas" (P. L. 90-222, Sec. 123 (a) (5)) of high unemployment, the Labor Department announced that $100 million in "recouped" and "unspent" EOA and MDTA funds were being set aside to establish Concentrated Employment Programs in twenty-two areas.

The Design

The central concept of CEP was to provide a single base in targeted communities from which the area's manpower work and training programs could be planned and delivered. CEPs were underway when the CWTP was authorized, and there were several advantages for the

Department of Labor in focusing its efforts for comprehensive man-power programs on CEP and leaving the CWTP dormant. The Department of Labor had explicit authority to administer the program, eliminating the need for lengthy negotiations with OEO over who should be in charge. Initially, no real debate over prime sponsorship developed since the CAAs were the institutions already in place serving the same people for whom CEP was envisaged. Still another advantage for CEP was the ability of the Department of Labor to channel MDTA funds into the programs and to call on the employment service to provide counseling, placement, and job development assistance to the CEPs. Generally, these monies and services had not been available to antipoverty agencies.

Eighty-two CEP contracts were in effect at the beginning of 1973: sixty-eight urban and fourteen rural. Over half of the CEPs were sponsored by CAAs; many of the others were contracted through city or county government:

Total	*82*
Community Action Agencies	47
City and/or county government	25
City and CAA	1
State agencies (all rural CEPs):	6
Employment service	(4)
Governor	(1)
Vocational Education Agency	(1)
Miscellaneous nonprofit organizations	3

The original CEP design called for services to be delivered to a target area of 50,000 and 150,000 people. The rationale for the restriction was that the limited resources would have the most visible impact if they were concentrated. In 1969, the population limit was revised downward to 50,000. After that, however, the target area concept took a backseat to the idea of comprehensive citywide programs. By the beginning of 1973, eighteen cities had expanded their CEP service area to include entire cities or counties.

Only persons living in poverty were eligible to enroll in a CEP, but most inner city residents qualified. In several areas with limited minority populations, it was necessary to expand the CEP boundaries in order to find enough persons to fill all available slots. The CEPs did not necessarily serve only those persons who experienced the severest difficulties in becoming gainfully employed. In fact, the revised 1969 guidelines required that those who could not be expected to complete the program, such as addicts, alcoholics, and the mentally and physically handicapped, should be referred to another appropriate agency.

CEPs were to have flexibility in planning programs to suit their needs. In practice, categorical contracting was most often the rule. Likewise, the idea that this new program could coordinate other community manpower programs was unrealistic. In most cases, CEP did not bring innovations in the use of the area's manpower funds or even their consolidation, but simply added manpower dollars to the CAA budgets and overlaid a new coordinating device on the manpower system that was already in place.

The services of the District of Columbia CEP are typical. Outreach centers established in poverty neighborhoods are usually the enrollee's point of entry. Once accepted, enrollees are given an orientation to the program and their needs are assessed by interviewers and counselors. Most are assigned first to basic education or vocational training either at the city skills center or one of the city's vocational education sites; the District's antipoverty agency, the United Planning Organization, which sponsors CEP, purchases these slots. After completing training, the enrollee may be placed directly in a job, in on-the-job training through the city's JOBS program, or in a subsidized Public Service Careers or Neighborhood Youth Corps position, a program also administered by UPO.

The difficult task for the planners and administrators of CEPs has been to move their enrollees through such a series of manpower services, losing as little time as possible between program components. CEP was not intended to be, literally, a one-stop service center where the client could shop for the distinct types of services he wanted, but a deliverer of an uninterrupted sequence of services, each building up the enrollee's employability.

Social Services

Most CEPs could not afford to offer all the supportive and follow-up services mentioned in the Economic Opportunity Act—health, counseling, day care, transportation, and others. The District of Columbia CEP, for example, spent 2 percent of its budget on health care and 8 percent on day care. Two-week orientation programs were generally available, and some personal counseling may have found its way into them or into the vocational counseling done by the employability development teams. To make their employment and training efforts truly comprehensive, CEPs were encouraged to add social services to their programs either through coordination with social service activities funded by the CAA or those provided by other public and private social welfare organizations.

Only a few CEPs were able to negotiate for grants which included subsidies for day care, transportation, legal aid, or medical examinations. Instead, they depended on being able to turn to other agencies which would serve CEP enrollees without charge or below cost. As spartan as the provision of these supportive services has been in CEP, it was superior to that offered in any other manpower program, with the exception of WIN.[36] Supportive services were optional in JOBS contracts, for example, and MDTA trainees were likely to receive only transportation allowances and possibly a medical examination.

CEP and Employers

The involvement of the business community was another element of a comprehensive program planned by CEP, but job development activities in CEP projects were generally adjudged to be weak. To bolster these activities, CEP enrollees were given priority in the National Alliance of Businessman's JOBS program, but this did little to improve relations between the CEPs and the business community. The natural tendency was for employers, when thrown into the manpower system, to drift toward the establishment agencies like the employment service rather than the community action organizations.[37] During fiscal year 1973, CEP clients filled only 3400 of the 51,500 JOBS slots.[38]

Occasionally, however, CEP and the business community were able to work together. In Cleveland a nonprofit organization, AIM-JOBS, was created especially to run the CEP program. The impetus came from private employers, who, since the formation of the Businessmen's Interracial Committee three years earlier, had been involved in a variety of activities to improve city housing, education, and race relations. The influence of private employers was apparent in the efforts of Cleveland's CEP to induce private businesses to locate facilities in ghetto neighborhoods by offering special manpower services to the employees they hired.

At the outset, the Cleveland CEP was heavily criticized by employers and administrators of other manpower programs. Even employers who cooperated with the CEP protested the addition of another team of job developers contacting them for job openings, and they became discouraged with the poor performance of AIM graduates on the job. Other manpower agencies complained that AIM-JOBS was offering services which they already were delivering.

Despite the initial controversies, the Cleveland CEP became a member of the city manpower establishment and retained its orientation toward private employers. During 1974, its budget of $3.5 million was the largest of any manpower program in the city. Only a fourth of the budget was spent on training because AIM-JOBS felt pressured to produce more placements in order to survive. Job development became the top priority, and AIM's job developers were assisted by lay people from local businesses recruited by the city's National Alliance of Businessmen. Graduates of AIM training received priority.

Prior to the passage of CETA, AIM-JOBS had begun to consolidate its training programs in-house and to spend less of its funds in subcontracts with other city manpower agencies. The strategy was contrary to the CEP mission of coordinating and utilizing services available from other manpower agencies, but AIM was afraid to lose control of manpower funds during a period when an economic downturn was hurting its success in placing the disadvantaged. It is likely that AIM will continue to specialize in job development. Under CETA, CEPs must seek allocations from the mayor and will have to compete to maintain their role as deliverers of comprehensive manpower services.

Enriching the CEP Design

The early CEP record was poor, and the confusion that surrounded their records of placements and costs was chalked up to poor management.[39] As a result, in 1969 the Department of Labor urged the revision of the CEP program by imposing two changes in the delivery of services. Guidelines required that Employability Development Teams (EDT) be introduced and that CEP "manpower services" components be subcontracted to the local employment service.

The EDT approach had been used in the Work Incentive program and in the Employment Service's Human Resources Development program. Teams consisting of a vocational counselor, a work training assistant, a job development specialist, a job "coach," and a clerical assistant were assigned a caseload of enrollees. The members of the team were supposed to offer personal assistance to the enrollees as needed. [40] In practice, however, Employability Development Teams did not operate as units and caseloads were so large, frequently in excess of 200, as to preclude close relationships with the clients. [41] Team plans were often ill-defined and usually reflected whatever services the CEP had to offer. Usually, counseling sessions and contacts with the client lagged after the initial assessment. The breakdown in team design was compounded by a lack of training available to the staff.

One major problem that the team approach did not solve was the lag that occurred between an enrollee's completion of one step in the employability development plan and the next. In CEP terminology, about 56,540 times during fiscal year 1973, one of the 109,500 clients who participated in some way in CEP was placed in "holding" status. No estimate is available of how many clients were on waiting lists more than once during the year or how long each waited, but it is clear that the incidence of holding was directly related to terminations from the program. Over half of all CEP dropouts left the program while "holding." [42] The sources of these lags appear to be weaknesses in the ability of Employability Development Teams to follow their caseloads through sequential services and in overall CEP job development.

The 1969 administrative changes also called on CEPs to subcontract with the employment service for the delivery of the "manpower services package." This controversial change was to give the employment service responsibility for a "package" which included outreach, intake, orientation, assessment and counseling, coaching, referral to employability development services, referral to supportive services, job development, placement, and follow-up. [43] This federal reaction to poor CEP management and performance was so severe that if compliance had been fully achieved, CEP sponsors would have been stripped of nearly all direct authority over most CEP operations. The order alluded to a shared responsibility that seemed infeasible, if not contradictory. The CEP sponsor would retain overall management while the employment service would have administrative control over the work of Employability Development Teams.

CEP sponsors, of course, strongly opposed the enlarged role of the employment service. Claiming that they represented the interests of the poor, CEP directors charged the Department of Labor with violating the philosophy of community action by turning authority over to the employment service which, in their opinion, had a deplorable reputation in serving the poor.[44] For their part, the employment service agencies felt that their new responsibility for delivering CEP manpower services eliminated CAAs' encroachment on their rightful turf. They believed that established agencies had a comparative advantage in management and that a more appropriate role for CAAs was advocacy of the poor and not administering programs for them.

Although the potential for an employment service-CEP showdown was heightened by the order, coordination problems were not universal. Although some CEPs opposed the new rules and fought them in the courts, by 1973, on the whole, CEPs and public employment offices lived in a state of peaceful coexistence. In most cases, the CEPs subcontracted manpower services to the employment service, while the employment service supported CEP goals for helping the disadvantaged. Under CETA, the threat to community action comes from the city hall or county courthouse, not the state employment service, and it is likely that many employment services will continue to subcontract for manpower services.

The Milwaukee and Albuquerque CEPs provide useful histories of the CEP maturation process. The Social Development Commission, Milwaukee County's community action agency, became the CEP sponsor in 1967. The agency's first CEP director adopted an aggressive posture in the community and openly criticized the Metropolitan Milwaukee Association of Commerce (the NAB-JOBS sponsor), the Department of Labor, and the city hall-sponsored Model Cities Program, of which CEP was to be the manpower arm, as racist. The CEP demanded that Milwaukee employers lower their requirements for employment to hire more inner city residents. The clash with employers and the racism charges prevented cooperation with the Association of Commerce's NAB-JOBS program.

When the Wisconsin State Employment Service took over CEP's job development and placement function in 1970, the chairman of the CEP board representing target area residents took the case to federal court. By 1972, when an appellate court eventually ruled that the shift of duties violated the Economic Opportunity Act's requirement of citizen participation in planning antipoverty programs, the CEP and the employment service had negotiated a compromise that allowed the program to continue. The community action agency subcontracted with the employment service for the "manpower services" and with the CEP resident board for supportive services and training.

In Milwaukee the abandonment of the goals of comprehensive services and of citizen participation, in large part due to Labor Department pressure, left the CEP a categorical program. Although its funds were pared by over one-half between 1967 and 1973, it remained the largest single program in Milwaukee. Ironically, after the budget cuts, staff reductions, and the subcontract with the employment service, the Milwaukee CEP's success as judged by the traditional standards of placements and costs showed considerable improvement.

The Albuquerque CEP also got off to a bad start, according to researchers Patrick H. McNamara and Gloria Griffin-Mallory. A self-evaluation by the CEP staff in Albuquerque and one by the Department of Labor regional office in 1969 found that during its first year its administration was deficient and recordkeeping inaccurate. CEP duplicated services available elsewhere in the city. In response to the Labor Department's demand for corrective action, the Albuquerque CEP hired more counselors and "coaches" to help guide the clients through to placement, and administrative steps were taken to bring the management problems under control.

This reform apparently paid off. A review by the Manpower Administration regional office three years later concluded that the program had achieved fiscal responsibility and was monitoring enrollees satisfactorily. Moreover, Albuquerque's CEP had established a good working relationship with the local employment service, a conflict that many other CEPs faced. Yet the Albuquerque CEP continued to experience difficulties in placing many enrollees, and its reputation for poor performance, shared by other CEPs, lingered; in part, the reason was that optimistic rhetoric never lived up to the harsh realities of placing ghetto residents in jobs. The problems of overblown expectations were exacerbated by hostilities in some areas between CEP sponsors, usually the antipoverty agencies, and local elected officials and traditional manpower agencies whose activities they were to coordinate.

CEP Lessons

The CEP program has provided the Department of Labor with its most extensive experience with a multifaceted manpower program. As more CEPs stretched their target areas to include entire cities or counties, CEPs moved away from representing "concentrated," that is, geographically limited, employment programs. The "concentrated" concept was deceptive anyway since annual budgets were usually too small to make any noticeable impact. For example, the $3.5 million CEP budget for the two targeted areas in Milwaukee represented only $35 per resident in 1973 or less than $200 for each inner city resident counted in the city's universe of need. The cost per successful placement of the Milwaukee CEP was $5300.

However, CEP has retained its distinction as one of the three manpower systems able to provide more than mere training and referral to jobs. Another delivery system, WIN, is limited to welfare recipients. The third, the employment service, has enjoyed a unique position legislatively and administratively and has been assigned so many duties that it has not been directly responsible for providing a full range of manpower services to disadvantaged persons. Only CEP provides a preview of the types of comprehensive manpower programs that might emerge under CETA, provided funds are adequate.

Although many CEPs have gained valuable experience in organizing comprehensive services, the most important lesson of the CEP experience was that mandating coordination among manpower program agents will not assure comprehensive planning and programming at the local level. It took specific legislative authority to consolidate MDTA and EOA programs, and, even with this, the involvement of the employment service will continue to be subject to local negotiations. It is not clear that the new legislative mandate will achieve more integrated and comprehensive manpower programs than CEP, or that it will even mean more efficient management.

CEP's mandate to include a variety of supportive services in its delivery sequences did set in motion efforts to arrange for the provision of these services to CEP clients by other agencies. Under CETA, funds to operate their own day care centers, or to hire legal or medical consultants, will continue to be limited and good relations between manpower sponsors and other agencies will be critical. Supportive services are needed by the whole community, not just manpower program enrollees, and it is beyond the abilities and resources of manpower programs to solve the social problems of their enrollees.[45] The CEP experience will be an important contribution to the planning of the comprehensive manpower programs.

A final mandate, that to bring business into close cooperation with

CEP, was generally unsuccessful. CEP's association with community action and poor, black enrollees was not attractive to employers. Compounding CEP job development problems was the reduction in potential job openings throughout the economy.

CEP's contributions to the reform of manpower planning and programming may appear small, and its success in many aspects of the program may appear questionable. However, in designing and implementing CEPs, the Department of Labor developed a basic plan for the operation of comprehensive manpower programs at the local level. It was one of the bases on which the Nixon administration began to build in shifting manpower authority to elected officials.

Momentum for Manpower Reform

Whatever the weaknesses of the CAMPS and CEPs, these exercises provided federal policymakers the insights for charting the direction of changes in manpower planning and programming.[46] But progress was slow as proposed manpower reform legislation became mired in political controversy.

Manpower Reform Stalls in Congress

Two bills dealing with manpower reform were introduced during the spring of 1969 by Congressmen William A. Steiger and James G. O'Hara. Both favored decategorized manpower services, but they differed on the agents to whom authority over manpower efforts should be delegated. Steiger's bill envisaged the governors as prime sponsors, conducting planning on a statewide basis, while under O'Hara's proposal, the Secretary of Labor would have retained tight control over the use of funds.

These bills were joined in August 1969 by the administration's Manpower Training Act, cosponsored by Representative William Ayres and Senator Jacob Javits. The bill would have combined MDTA and EOA manpower programs (except for the Job Corps) under a single authority. Governors would have been given the responsibilities for developing the initial state plan, for establishing a state comprehensive manpower agency, and for designating local prime sponsors who, in turn, would prepare community manpower plans.

The Employment and Manpower Act of 1970 that won congressional approval included much of the intent of the administration proposal. States, cities with a population of over 75,000 and counties of 100,000, or any combination of government units of over 100,000 persons could become prime sponsors. However, the categorical work and training programs were retained and a few new ones were added. Perhaps most objectionable to the administration was the provision for public service employment. The bill was vetoed by President Nixon who criticized its failure to decategorize manpower programs and its inclusion of "WPA" public service jobs.

A similar manpower reform bill was reintroduced in 1971. It was countered with another administration bill which made even clearer the President's notion of "New Federalism." Earlier manpower reform proposals provided for shared authority among federal, state, and local sponsors, leaving the Department of Labor a significant role in manpower planning and the monitoring of programs as well as a slice of funds for federally designated activities. The administration's "manpower revenue sharing" called for grants by formula to state and local governments, whose use of money would not get prior approval by the Department of Labor. Except for distributing the funds, federal presence in manpower efforts was to dwindle to a minimum.

No manpower reform bill emerged from the 92nd Congress. Support for manpower reform waned, as it became clear how radically the administration proposed to shift power away from Congress and the federal executive departments under revenue sharing. However, in the interim, a public service employment program, the Emergency Employment Act of 1971, did become law. It signaled the acceptance of transitional public employment to combat high unemployment. The law also decentralized funds to elected officials.

Pilot Comprehensive Manpower Programs

With manpower reform legislation bogged down in Congress, the Department of Labor sought to experiment with "decategorized" and "decentralized" manpower administration. But effective experimentation required the active cooperation of several executive agencies. The Department of Labor sought agreement from OEO to jointly designate demonstration projects to test the results of public (and thus less fragmented) sponsorship. Nineteen areas were selected where the local CAA was already a public agency or where no CAA existed. OEO had resisted the Department of Labor's previous attempts to replace CAAs with public agencies (specifically the state employment service) as prime sponsors, but by May 1971 the antipoverty agency agreed to the pilot projects.

The Department of Labor moved slowly to implement these projects, and it took prodding by Congress. Persuaded of the desirability to experiment with greater local control over manpower funds, the House and Senate Appropriations subcommittees specifically urged the approval of pilot projects. The House subcommittee stated that it would expect the Labor Department to work with OEO and HEW "to revise their operating budgets with the goal in mind of reducing or eliminating categorical distinctions in order to provide flexible bloc grants" to the states or local governments that would sponsor the pilot programs.[47] Since both the MDTA and the EOA included provision for experimentation and demonstration projects, there were no legislative barriers to trial "comprehensive manpower programs."

The pilot comprehensive manpower program (CMP) was announced by the Department of Labor in December 1972. Nine areas were selected as the first-round pilot CMP projects: the states of New Hampshire, South Carolina, and Utah; Luzerne County, Pennsylvania; and the metropolitan areas of Albuquerque, Hartford, Omaha, Miami (Dade County), and Seattle.

The pilot areas were in no way newcomers to the manpower scene and were selected because of their interest and evidenced capabilities. Albuquerque, for example, had a Washington-trained manpower director, David Rusk, and Utah's governor and state planning council representatives had been actively promoting manpower reform since 1969 with the guidance of manpower experts Garth L. Mangum and R. Thayne Robson. Luzerne County is represented in Congress by Daniel J. Flood, chairman of the appropriations subcommittee responsible for the Labor and HEW budgets.

Yet while federal officials and those in the pilot areas talked glibly of decategorization and decentralization, the catchwords of manpower reform, a closer look reveals only marginal changes in the manpower system at the test sites. Consolidation rather than decategorization aptly described the improvements in program administration. Decentralization of authority to local officials for planning and carrying out CMP grants meant that control of MDTA and EOA manpower dollars was transferred to a single prime sponsor who was the chief elected official (or consortium of officials). However, subcontracts to former prime sponsors continued to give the system much of its former categorical flavor. And, despite the relaxation of administrative guidelines, federal influence continued to be considerable.

Albuquerque's experience illustrates these problems. Consolidation of the area's manpower programs began with the efforts of the CEP director and city officials to transfer CEP sponsorship from the community action agency to the city. The regional OEO office protested the loss of this $1.8 million program, and it took the persuasive powers of local community action officials to convince the regional office that city and county officials had plans to give the local CAA a continued role in manpower. The negotiations concluded in December 1971 and led to an agreement between the city and surrounding Bernalillo County that designated the city manager's office to assume prime sponsorship of the area's manpower programs. Later in 1972, the city's Model Cities program was transferred to the Office of Manpower Programs (OMP), which had been created to house CMP activities. The school system was willing to let the new manpower office assume prime sponsorship responsibilities for the Neighborhood Youth Corps programs, but continued to operate them.

Folding MDTA-institutional and WIN programs into the CMP was a more difficult task. In order to place the former under OMP wings, MDTA regulations required that the state vocational education agency and the employment service agree to transfer funds to the Albuquerque OMP, which would then disburse them to local projects. These arrangements were made readily, but to assume sponsorship of WIN, OMP officials had to negotiate with the governor of New Mexico and his planning council to transfer the program from employment service hands. The Albuquerque manpower officials eventually convinced the state planners that the employment service would not really lose the program because OMP intended to subcontract with the local employment service for services to WIN clients. Once the planners agreed, the governor was persuaded to override the protests of the employment service and allow Albuquerque to include WIN in its CMP. In sum, OMP assumed the local administrative responsibilities for both MDTA and WIN, but the subcontracting arrangements left the programs readily identifiable categorical efforts.

The design of the Albuquerque CMP delivery system was an expanded version of CEP. Five outreach centers were established staffed with employment service personnel. Enrollees were distributed among categorical programs, depending on their eligibility and needs. By the end of 1973, OMP administered all programs covered by CETA in addition to WIN. Consolidation could not bring decategorization, but it did result in administrative savings through the reduction of excessive staff. By the end of 1973, manpower staff had been cut from sixty-four to thirty-five, a savings of $250,000 annually.

Among the other pilot CMPs, the effort to consolidate programs was less extensive than in Albuquerque, but they contributed a variety of multijurisdictional arrangements. Luzerne County, the CMP sponsor, is the only governmental unit in the county eligible to receive funds under CETA. Dade County has a metropolitan government, combining at least three potential sponsors into one. In the Seattle area, two counties and seven cities formed a consortium of governments solely to act as the manpower prime sponsor. Utah's statewide plan is composed of the plans submitted by seven multi-county associations of government. If the state had been unable to negotiate Salt Lake City's voluntary submission to statewide prime sponsorship, the state would have been planning for only a few smaller cities and sparsely populated rural areas.

In general, consolidated funding did not change the identities of local program operators. Dade County proposed open bidding for manpower service contracts, but so far competition has taken the form of lobbying with planning councils and elected officials. At all CMP sites, community action agencies, the employment service, school systems, and special interest groups continued to operate many programs. These early experiences dim prospects that CETA's consolidated funding will bring with it consolidated program operations. On the bright side, however, Albuquerque, as noted, demonstrated that substantial reductions in administrative costs could be made by centralizing recordkeeping and fiscal operations.

Given more freedom to set their priorites and allocate funds, the CMPs did make some changes. Dade County planners were able to substantiate their claim that Vietnam Era veterans did not constitute a significant enough group to warrant priority status. In Albuquerque, planners bravely proposed to reduce unemployment to 3.5 percent, raise three of every four poor families out of poverty, and increase median family income to the national average by concentrating manpower efforts on youth and women—target groups somewhat less restrictive than federal priorities: veterans, welfare recipients, and minority youth.

Two caveats must be set forth before generalizing about the contributions of the CMP to comprehensive manpower reform. First, the nine CMP jurisdictions were not representative of the political and administrative arrangements encountered in other jurisdictions qualified to act as prime sponsors of manpower efforts. Absent from the CMP experience was the situation where a city and its surrounding county (or counties) would both become eligible to sponsor manpower programs. In that situation a conflict between the ideal of planning for the labor market and planning by political jurisdictions is inevitable. Also missing from among the CMP state pilots was a state in which the majority of the population lives in metropolitan areas.[48]

Second, while the CMPs were offered an opportunity to exercise local judgments as to what programs and prime sponsors should be included in their manpower system, activities were constrained by the legislative requirements of the MDTA and the EOA. The Labor Department could relax administrative requirements by administrative fiat but could not absolve the states and localities of the necessity to account for MDTA and EOA expenditures separately.

Each pilot project has demonstrated new approaches to some aspect of the administration, planning, or operation of manpower programs. However, with the possible exceptions of Utah and Albuquerque, the programs have not been in operation long enough to allow assessment of the outcomes of any experiments. To recommend the adoption of any particular design by other cities, counties, or states might be ill-advised and, perhaps, would only discourage them from making their own contributions.

The CMPs have had the advantage of intense federal attention which will not be feasible when the Labor Department must monitor the nearly 500 CETA sponsors. Left alone, changes in other areas are likely to come gradually. It will be wiser, then, to look at the initial experience under the new law without rose-colored glasses and refrain from expecting its mandate to create comprehensive manpower programs to bring greater changes than can reasonably be expected.

A Workable Compromise:
The Comprehensive Employment and Training Act

While the 1973 manpower legislation proposals were winding their way through Congress, the Labor Department was considering funding a new round of CMP projects. The signing of CETA on December 28, 1973 intervened, and the attempted reform of manpower programs through administrative actions gave way to legislative sanction. The law set forth a structure with many of the elements advocated by manpower reformers, but it was a far cry from the administration's original manpower revenue sharing proposals.

CETA consists of six titles. The first provides grants to states and localities for a variety of manpower services (Table 3). The second provides additional funds for public service employment programs in areas where unemployment is above 6.5 percent, though eligible communities can use the funds for other manpower programs. Other titles outline federal responsibilities for special target groups including Indians, migrant workers, and disadvantaged youth and establish requirements for federal research and evaluation. The Job Corps is retained in a separate title, and another mandates the establishment of a National Commission for Manpower Policy.

Decentralization

What is new in CETA is not the mandate to fund comprehensive manpower programs through a single prime sponsor, but a compromise solution to intergovernmental conflicts and to disputes over the proper role of community-based organizations. A part of the solution is embodied in the formula-funding mechanism for Title I. Most grants for manpower services will be made to general governments: states, localities representing over 100,000 people, and combinations of local jurisdictions of which at least one represents over 100,000 people. The Department of Labor may designate general governments in needy areas regardless of size if they are capable of providing manpower services; eleven such areas will be eligible in fiscal 1975. The only nongovernmental prime sponsors that the Department of Labor may fund are rural CEPs which have proved their effectiveness in serving high unemployment areas. Four rural CEPs, in eastern Kentucky, Wisconsin, Minnesota, and Montana, will sponsor CETA programs.

By funding "general governments," not "elected officials," the law may help clarify the roles of elected mayors and city managers. The problems of shifting power to weak mayors in cities where the city manager has administrative powers had first come to light during fiscal

Table 3. Administration's Recommended Distribution of CETA Funds, Fiscal 1975 (millions).

Title	Funds
Total	$2050.0
I: Comprehensive Manpower Programs	1319.0
Grants to states and localities by formula	1055.2
State manpower services councils	10.6
State funds for statewide programs	52.7
Vocational education incentives	66.0
Multijurisdictional incentives	66.0
Secretary of Labor discretionary funds	68.5
II: Public Employment Programs	350.0
Grants to states and localities	280.0
Secretary of Labor discretionary funds	70.0
III: Federal Programs	210.0
Indians	42.2
Migrants	52.7
Other national programs	72.6
Research and development, technical assistance, evaluation and labor market information	42.5
IV: Job Corps	171.0

Source: Manpower Information Service, *Reference File* (Washington: Bureau of National Affairs), p. 21:1021

year 1972 when HUD granted elected officials in twenty cities authority to vary the way their Model Cities funds were spent. Seven of every ten cities with populations of over 100,000 have a city manager government.[49] San Diego is typical. San Diego's mayor heads the legislative branch (the city council), and the city manager has the administrative powers. To conform with the Department of Labor's 1971 regulations giving planning authority to elected officials, San Diego's mayor claimed the manpower planning council and appointed its members. His approval was required on the plans, and he appointed an evaluation committee to review it. The staff which prepared the plan, however, was housed in the city Human Resources Department and reported to the city manager, not the mayor, who is forbidden from issuing directives to city departments.

Although the law established up to a 10 percent bonus to be allocated to areas joining forces for prime sponsorship, it offers little incentive to foster cooperation in program implementation. In approximately one-fourth of the SMSAs, more than one prime sponsor will be eligible. No doubt, combinations will run the gamut from elaborate consortium arrangements to independence among sponsors in the same labor market area. The four eligible jurisdictions in the Cleveland area plus an additional county have laid aside their political differences in favor of a consortium, for example. But the counties outside the District of Columbia have opted for both independent planning and operations. How other jurisdictions will weigh the political and financial advantages of multijurisdictional arrangements is uncertain. Many areas may take a wait-and-see attitude toward multijurisdictional schemes while other proposals to decentralize community development and education programs are debated.

The State's Role

In setting the size of eligible local prime sponsors at 100,000 population, CETA will serve two-thirds of the population through city and county sponsors. The rest will be covered by state programs. The distribution of funds will likely be in the same proportion.[50]

A special state and local coordinating device, the state manpower services council, is authorized by the law. It gives governors an added role in state manpower affairs beyond their role as prime sponsors for areas not qualified to act as prime sponsors. A Senate proposal would have given governors a larger share of manpower funds and potentially greater leverage over the manpower programs of local sponsors, but CETA trimmed the share of funds that statehouses will receive. And, the Act requires that local officials constitute a third of the state manpower services council membership.

Although the council is charged with the responsibility of coordinating state and local programs, its mandates to review the plans submitted by each sponsor and those of the state agencies, to monitor the programs, and to report annually to the governor leave the councils without real authority to modify the operations of local sponsors or the state agencies. And, as was evident from the CAMPS' experience, assembling the state agency representatives at the same table with representatives of other manpower programs will not ensure successful integration of state agency programs in the manpower system. Lacking a role in the budget process, the state manpower services councils are left with only the uncertain powers of persuasion and an even more doubtful impact that might occur as a result of releasing public reports.

There are advantages for local prime sponsors to use state services, not the least of which is that they may be available without cost. Moreover, 4 percent of comprehensive manpower funds, or about $53 million in fiscal 1975 assuming Congress adopts the administration budget proposals, can be provided to governors for statewide manpower services which may include employment services, training, or the development of labor market information. The governors' use of these funds will be the critical test of their willingness and ability to apply the services of their state agencies to the needs of local sponsors.

There is also a special "carrot" in the law to encourage the state vocational educators to work with the prime sponsors. The Department of Labor is able to make special grants up to 5 percent of Title I funds to the governors to provide vocational services where the state vocational education agency and the prime sponsor have jointly agreed that additional services are needed. About $66 million will be available for these programs in fiscal 1975. Success with this experiment might open wider the options for community manpower planners.

Decategorization

The Comprehensive Employment and Training Act allows designated sponsors to develop their own mix of manpower programs, and sharply curtails federal interference with the choice of activities. The decategorization, however, is not as complete as the administration originally intended. It is recommended that programs of demonstrated effectiveness be retained by sponsors, and plans for institutional skill training programs must give priority consideration to the utilization of existing MDTA skills centers. There is a separate title, with separate guidelines and reporting requirements, for public employment programs in areas where the unemployment rate has been 6.5 percent or more for three consecutive months. However, the sponsors can shift those funds to other types of programs as long as they continue to serve people in the high unemployment area.

Congress also did not ignore the target groups whose needs were emphasized during the past decade. The federal government may retain part of the appropriation to operate programs to supplement those of local sponsors for youth, older workers, persons with limited English-speaking ability, inmates in correctional institutions, Indians, and migrant workers. The Job Corps is retained under national administration. Therefore, of the $2.1 billion proposed appropriation for fiscal 1975, more than one-third will be authorized categorically: $350 million for public employment, approximately $210 million for national target group programs and support activities, $171 million for the Job Corps, and $66 million for vocational education.

Slicing the Pie

Categorical funding aside, the basic grants to states and localities for manpower services will be distributed according to a weighted, three-part formula: 50 percent according to the previous year's allotment, 37.5 percent based on the number of unemployed, and 12.5 percent based on the number of adults in families with annual incomes below $7000 (adjusting for cost-of-living increases since 1969). Areas which previously received manpower funds cannot be reduced to less than 90 percent or increased to over 150 percent of the funds they received in the preceding year. The low budget factors (rather than poverty line) and the large weight given to the unemployment rate tend to favor metropolitan areas where unemployment is more concentrated and where income tends to be higher than in rural areas. The immediate impact, however, is to drain manpower funds from the central cities by giving equal status to many newly eligible suburban jurisdictions without severe manpower problems.

Whether the formula will result in a more equitable distribution of funds than under the less precise system of categorical grants is difficult to predict. The emphasis on treating concentrated pockets of poverty has given way to serving a proportional number of the poor and unemployed in every political jurisdiction. In large part, the heavy weight given to unemployment is a recognition that it is the best available statistic, not that it is a better measure of need than the poverty criteria. In any event, the data used will probably be a year old and of questionable validity when collected. Only the provision allocating public employment funds in areas where unemployment rises above 6.5 percent for three consecutive months attempts to respond more rapidly to changing economic conditions.

Even though the Labor Department must maintain each prime sponsor's first year's funding at 90 percent of previous year's allocations under MDTA and EOA, the sponsors will still be facing larger overall reductions in the real value of their budgets. Approximately $2.6 billion was expended for the programs covered by CETA in fiscal 1973. Adjusted for increased costs, the $2.05 billion appropriations requested by the administration for fiscal 1975 will hardly stretch as far as the estimated $1.6 billion spent on MDTA and EOA manpower activities in 1973, excluding the $1 billion expended on public employment.

A Federal Role

Besides its role in administering programs to target groups, the federal government remains the steward of the manpower grants. All plans submitted by states and localities must be approved by federal officials. Those officials are likely to rubber stamp each plan and withhold approval only in cases of clear violations or strongly substantiated allegations of abuse. The comments submitted by governors and other local officials, the reports of the manpower services councils, and federal evaluations will provide supplementary information on the plans' adequacies and how well services are performed.

The responsibility for training and guiding sponsors will be federal, and, given the large number of newly endowed jurisdictions, this will be an important function. Over the past several years, there has been a marked shift of federal staff from Washington to the regional offices to provide the needed services. But pressures from the Office of Management and Budget to maintain only skeleton federal administrative support may not allow the regional offices to expand their activities beyond the ability to give cursory help to local sponsors.

A trimming down of the federal structure may act to undermine a basic source of strength in the manpower system. The law retains federal research, evaluation, and development functions. Management information systems, labor market information, and computerized job matching efforts will continue under federal auspices and will be expanded to include CETA's required development of data on unemployment, underemployment, and demand for labor by states, local and poverty areas, as well as methods to measure nationwide the economic adequacy of employment and earnings. These mandates plus the administrative structure necessary to disperse federal program responsibilities necessitate keeping the federal manpower establishment in place. Sharp cuts in federal manpower personnel are a source of deep concern to advocates of a truly federal manpower system.

The "New" Manpower System?

Certainly the Comprehensive Employment and Training Act will not cure all the ills of the "old" manpower system. Planning and budgeting are at long last placed under a single authority, and the grant process may be simplified. But it is not at all clear that the setting of priorities and control over funds by elected state and local officials or their designated bureaucrats, rather than by their federal counterparts, will contribute to a more effective manpower system. The new system also provides for a wider geographic distribution of funds, but as long as needs exceed the limited resources, the addition of areas to be served will only proliferate inadequate efforts rather than help those whose needs are greatest.

Will the manpower system change and will services improve? There will continue to be a variety of subcontractors, and the goal of a sequential delivery of services or a one-stop service center may be no nearer. The employment service, the Work Incentive program, state vocational rehabilitation and the largest portion of vocational education programs are still not integrated into the system. It is neither possible nor desirable to eliminate special interests and their representatives. Whatever reorganizations CETA will bring will not solve the tougher manpower issues—what strategies are the most effective for serving the unemployed, underemployed, poor, and minorities?

There is little reason to anticipate that CETA will result in improvement of services offered to clients. It is likely that manpower dollars under the new system will buy the same "bang for the buck." Although some administrative savings may occur, these are not likely to affect appreciably program efficiency. A new manpower law cannot by itself ameliorate the functioning of the labor market and facilitate the opening of employment opportunites for program clientele.

Chapter 5

The Outlook
for the Manpower System

The review of more than a decade of federal, state, and local experience in trying to rationalize the manpower system reveals gradual progress. The passage of the 1973 Comprehensive Employment and Training Act in many ways may seem to be a climax in the history of manpower organization and planning since it suggests workable solutions to the problems of intergovernmental relations and accommodations between public and private sponsors. The law provides a blueprint for integrating manpower planning and operations under the single auspices of public officials. However, the CETA "solution" will leave many outstanding problems and no doubt give rise to new problems.

Most significant is the fact that consolidation is incomplete. Given the closely guarded jurisdictional preserves of congressional committees, the designers of CETA could only include under its umbrella the funds authorized by the Manpower Development and Training Act and Economic Opportunity Act. These comprise just 40 percent of federally funded manpower outlays. In addition, the new law provides for the continued funding of public employment. But because so many pieces of the manpower puzzle are not covered by CETA, public officials seeking truly comprehensive programs will continue to grapple with the dilemma of coordinating institutions accountable to different authorities. And in the final analysis, even the most workable manpower system is not going to eliminate the categorical needs that brought about manpower programs.

Nonetheless, the state and local sponsors of manpower programs will have much greater freedom in putting the pieces of their manpower puzzle together as they see fit. Their past experiences, as reflected largely in this report through the eyes of the six Urban Observatory studies sponsored by the National League of Cities, indicate, however, that at the outset few far-reaching changes can be anticipated realistically, although selected achievements might be replicated. There have been diverse examples of effective and ineffective planning and coordination of programs, and preparations among local officials in advance of CETA vary. Based on the case studies, changing the thrust and direction of established institutions is an evolutionary process; one can only hope, but not expect, that the lofty goals of CETA will be realized.

Ready or Not

During the manpower reform debate, skeptics charged that state and local sponsors were ill-prepared to design and operate manpower programs and that many state and local officials would not be sensitive to the needs of the disadvantaged. Presently, the word from the states and localities is that potential for good administration and planning is there, although, in some cases, expertise has not been fully developed. Areas which have received numerous federal manpower grants and which have long histories of involvement in other social programs have developed visible cadres of grant administrators, planners, job developers, instructors, and assorted other technicians who may have circulated among an area's social programs but who have gained an invaluable familiarity with the locality, its jobs, politicians, and other community leaders.

Capabilities are not evenly distributed, however. There are a number of areas with only very limited experience in planning or running manpower programs. Only within the last three years have some governors turned to the newly formed manpower offices as the official state representatives on labor market matters rather than rely upon the employment service, welfare and vocational education agencies. Excluding grants for public employment, most counties have become eligible for manpower funds for the first time under CETA. And even in some cities, like San Diego, researchers report that they are several years behind other metropolitan areas which have been more active in manpower. More time and resources will be needed for many jurisdictions to develop their manpower establishments, and it is unrealistic to anticipate overnight improvements resulting from the changes of the manpower guard.

Under CETA, the role of steward to the needs of the disadvantaged in the labor market has been passed from federal bureaucrats to state and local public officials. Critical eyes will be focusing on elected officials to see if they are attuned to the problems of their most disadvantaged citizens, the poor and minorities. During the past several years as program planning and administration were being brought under public control, private agencies representing the poor and certain minorities managed to maintain their position in local manpower either because of their proven performance or because they have exercised sufficient leverage to retain a piece of the action.

Nevertheless, the outlook for a sustained role for private groups representing the poor and minorities was dimming earlier this year when support for national funds for community action agencies and Model Cities agencies were due to lapse on June 30, 1974. CETA requires that local programs of demonstrated effectiveness be continued and that community-based groups be represented on planning councils, but local officials saw their hands tied. Aware that their shrinking local budgets would not be able to take up the slack, mayors and governors attempted to secure congressional support for renewed community action funds. The fate of viable separate institutions representing the poor and minorities may rest with Congress.

Continuing Needs and Shrinking Funds

During the 1960s, the nation was sensitized to the needs of the poor and minorities, and manpower programs were only one part of the response to the long-standing needs of urban areas. Central cities continue to be the areas of the most pressing and concentrated needs. In Milwaukee the difference between the inner city and other areas was most striking; the unemployment rate among poverty area residents was 11 percent compared with 1.5 percent in the rest of the city. The other studies also identify geographical areas of intense need—frequently the targets of major manpower projects. Several reported that the problem of geographic concentration of the poor, minorities, and the unskilled grew worse over the past decade as shifting residential patterns caused better paid workers to move to suburban areas. Skilled and professional jobs downtown are held by suburban residents, and in many cases, the growth of blue-collar employment opportunities has occurred outside the city.

Low earnings are as much a problem as unemployment; both are manifestations of labor market pathologies that manpower policymakers and planners must consider. The Albuquerque, Milwaukee, and the District of Columbia Urban Observatory studies have emphasized the potential of a manpower strategy that would try to raise family income through employment of secondary workers. None, however, is prepared to abandon the more traditional goals of utilizing manpower funds to upgrade low wage workers with skill training and to break down discriminatory barriers to employment.

CETA distributes funds by formula to all jurisdictions of 100,000 or more people. By qualifying suburban areas to sponsor manpower programs, CETA will broaden the geographic base of these efforts. This signals a policy shift from the days of the War on Poverty when the goal was to eradicate pockets of poverty by concentrating efforts in the areas of greatest need.

CETA also opens wider the range of people who may be served by manpower programs than the former system of categorical grants, which had tightly defined eligibility standards. Under CETA, the unemployed and underemployed, whatever their characteristics, are appropriate targets of manpower efforts. And, by raising the definition of low income to about $7000 a year for a family of four, CETA's standards allow sponsors greater flexibility in accepting the most job-ready from their traditional clienteles. It is conceivable that the proportion of the participants in manpower programs from the ranks of the most disadvantaged could decline.

The inadequacy of funding has been, and will remain, a perennial complaint of manpower planners and administrators. The pressure of retrenched federal manpower budgets combined with the loss of funding for other urban programs surfaced in the course of planning for fiscal 1974. That year the councils had their first crack at setting local priorities, but many found their decisionmaking limited to the unwelcome task of spreading budget cuts among existing efforts. Although CETA requires that each eligible jurisdiction receive at least 90 percent of the funds allocated in the previous year, it is obvious that without an increased manpower budget, the cities annually will face shrinking budgets. Inflation aside, in many cities, the CETA formula would have brought drastic reductions—from 45 percent in the District of Columbia to 23 percent in Albuquerque—if it were not for the so-called 90 percent "hold harmless" guarantee.

With the exception of a possible boosting of the ante for public employment, the outlook for a renewed growth of manpower expenditures is not altogether promising. But even additional public employment monies will absorb no more than a fraction of the unemployed, and manpower programs will be serving even smaller proportions of the needy.

An expanded definition of the eligible population and the wider geographic distribution of limited funds intensify the difficult problem that local decisionmakers must face in selecting the groups or individuals to be served. Boston researchers have summarized the dilemma of "whom to help" by identifying five groups needing manpower services. (1) Sponsors may choose to serve the most disadvantaged: those with little education, few skills, and the greatest likelihood of facing discrimination. Family heads whose dependents require additional attention may also be counted among the most disadvantaged. To help these groups requires efforts which have high costs, long duration, and probably low success rates. (2) In contrast, sponsors may choose to serve persons with fewer strikes against them and who could be helped at lower costs, thereby registering a high proportion of successful efforts. Many unemployed and low-wage workers as defined by CETA will fall into this category. (3) A third strategy might be to aim manpower programs at the groups constituting the largest proportion of the needy, for example, urban youth or, in some areas, urban whites. But with limited funds, their numbers among the needy could not be expected to be reduced substantially. (4) Conversely, intensified assistance to smaller groups, the non-English speaking, for example, would be more likely to yield a recognizable impact in well-defined neighborhoods. (5) Finally, another option might be to direct manpower efforts at socially volatile groups, like drug addicts or former offenders, at high per capita costs and little guarantee of success. Decisionmakers will be weighing these alternatives, and the strategy or combination of strategies they adopt will no doubt be a reflection of area politics as well as their values and willingness to accept risk.

The Manpower Investment

Since increased funding remains only a hope, program administrators and planners must set their sights to making the best out of what is available. Additional funds for experimentation are unlikely. Throughout the Urban Observatories, researchers concluded that employment and training programs pay off for those who participate. Milwaukee researchers, for example, looked at earnings of trainees prior to and after training and concluded that the programs pay for themselves after only a short period of time. Others, like those in Cleveland and the District of Columbia, singled out for praise several programs with successful records in placing their clientele in jobs. These results confirm the findings of the majority of manpower researchers over the years that manpower programs have been a worthwhile federal commitment. [51]

However, the methodology of measuring success is limited by its imprecision. Looking at the placement record of manpower programs, as most evaluators do, no claim can be made that the job resulted from the content of the program. But there are other benefits. The District of Columbia study, for example, pointed out the secondary benefits of manpower programs in that area, including income support from stipends, the employment of staff to operate programs, and the preference given to manpower clients in qualifying for supportive services. Total benefits must take into account longer-run changes—a client's work experience after he leaves the program. CETA requires a year-long follow-up on enrollees, which was a difficult task performed by few in the past. In the future, perhaps, valuable information on the work experience of the disadvantaged will be collected.

Local Adaptations

Directly or indirectly, all the Urban Observatory researchers were aware of a learning curve in local program management. Most areas have tried a variety of service components and were usually willing to contract for each new program as it was developed. Through experience, several sponsors have found ways to reduce costs, especially overhead, and to reorganize the program to make it more effective, in most cases measured by increasing job placement. But administrative savings were not universal, even though conventional wisdom asserts that good management means the elimination of duplicative programs. The results of the challenge by Boston's community action agency to the employment service and the school system suggest that there are benefits in rival programs with overlapping clients and services.

Federal policymakers have developed a series of models for serving different manpower needs, and despite criticisms that the categorical grants were too restrictive, many local sponsors adapted their programs to local conditions. In many cases, CEP and PEP gave sponsors more leeway than most. For example, the Cleveland CEP focused on job development because the agency administrators thought that was the best way to secure the cooperation of the city's employers while the Boston CEP was more sensitive to the failures of the traditional manpower agencies in serving minority communities and developed a variety of categorical skill training and employment programs to fill the gap. The District of Columbia PEP cooperated with other city manpower programs to place trainees in PEP slots. In Milwaukee, the city government adopted a first come, first serve policy without priorities for manpower clients. In none of the cases was one program or the other " the best" or using "the right" approach; each was finding locally acceptable solutions.

Such diversity suggests that states and localities have a lot to learn from each other; successes can sometimes be replicated, and savings can be accomplished by reducing the number of cases where the wheel is invented. Only within the past several years has funding of the public interest groups' manpower projects brought public sponsors together and promoted the exchange of ideas. These groups spent much time representing their constituents in Washington as manpower reform legislation was debated. They may continue to fill an important need by acting as a medium through which sponsors can communicate with each other directly. Sponsors are very likely to learn more from each other than from a study of Labor Department guidelines.

The Lessons of the Past

Over the past five years, manpower policymakers were gradually changing their focus from individual program developments to finding ways to decentralize authority to state and local officials. Two of the efforts basic to the development of decentralized planning and the design of comprehensive programs were CAMPS and CEP. Those who wrote CETA and drafted its regulations drew heavily on those experiences. As CETA is implemented, many of the policy issues raised by CAMPS and CEP will continue to be important.

Manpower Planning

The concept of state and local planning councils to coordinate manpower programs was sound and has been formally recognized in CETA.

Although CAMPS committees could do little to change manpower operations, they were a vital beginning, bringing together practitioners who worked on separate projects. Federal guidelines that shifted authority for CAMPS to elected officials and federal dollars to support their planning staffs nourished the interest of elected officials in manpower efforts.

The obstacles to fruitful planning persisted, however. This should not be at all surprising since much of the initial impetus for manpower planning was imposed from Washington. The apocryphal story about the mayor who was subjected to a sales pitch about the great potentials of CAMPS is suggestive. Having been persuaded by the federal officials' praise of CAMPS, the mayor inquired about the costs of the new device. When informed that Uncle Sam would pick up the tab, the mayor became even more enthusiastic and ordered three CAMPS for his city.

Though many elected officials were babes in the woods about the requirements and potentials of manpower planning, they and their staffs subsequently raised many questions concerning planning and offered options to resolve the emerging difficulties. State and local councils found the federal exhortation calling for comprehensive planning and the participation of business, labor, community, and client groups in addition to manpower professionals of little help, though they recognized the value of a broader-based planning council. The difficulty was to get the diverse groups to work together. Boston and Milwaukee researchers singled out the half-hearted involvement of local educators in manpower planning as a weakness, especially since their training and that of local manpower institutions overlap. Many were concerned about giving all three groups, clients, employers, and manpower professionals, equal representation among the council staff as well as among its members. Albuquerque has gone farther than most, perhaps, in opening planning to the widest participation by holding neighborhood meetings and contracting with the community action agency for independent evaluations.

A more troublesome question for local manpower planners is the problem of labor markets and political jurisdictions that do not coincide. Some will argue for federal intervention to define labor market areas and to sanction only one prime sponsor from each designated viable economic area regardless of conflicting political boundaries. CETA properly rejected this approach, and instead the Labor Department will be able to offer an incentive of up to 10 percent additional funding for planning by consortia covering substantial portions of labor market areas. The fact remains that many areas were able to work out satisfactory city-county relationships before CETA.

In the spring of 1973, Baltimore, for example, anticipated CETA's incentive for labor market consortia and became one of the first cities to negotiate an agreement for joint planning with five neighboring counties. There are also a variety of metropolitan governments, councils of government, and less formal arrangements—some including functions other than manpower and some more permanent than others. But where local politics are the bricks and mortar of such agreements, the federal mandate wrapped in a few dollars will not counteract the stresses of local politics. Most metropolitan areas prefer multijurisdictional planning; cities, especially, need access to suburban employers, but many of the newly endowed county sponsors may choose to test the water on their own rather than share a larger amount with neighboring jurisdictions.

As they gained experience, state and local planners protested that their effectiveness suffered from a paucity of available data to determine the number of persons in need of services, to forecast the demand for trainees, and to evaluate the impact of the programs. As a result, federal officials took several steps to adapt census data for local use, to assure that Labor Department data on local programs were available locally, and to experiment with local job vacancy measures and in-dustry-occupation matrices. CETA mandates the development of better methods to measure local labor force activities: timely local statistics on unemployment, underemployment, earnings, and house-hold budgets. Some local planners did attempt to experiment with fore-casting models and unearthed what local data sources they could. Both federal efforts and local expertise will have to be expanded if CETA's hopes of a national labor market information system appropriate for states and localities are to be fulfilled.

Program performance measurements were perhaps even harder to come by than local labor force data. A scrutiny of the available data led to criticism that program data collection was often spotty and inade-quate to meet evaluation needs and that some program administrators withheld much of the data they had collected. CETA maintains local reporting requirements to federal officials, but local sponsors are not confined to using just the reports prepared for the feds. As advisers to elected officials, planners have the opportunity to use their leverage to require fuller progress reports on program operations.

The mere collection of data, like little knowledge, may be a dangerous tool. Planners in the Urban Observatory cities indicated that the manpower data must be analyzed with care before they are applied for operational use. Placement costs, for example, are superficially sound performance criteria but they tend to encourage "creaming"—serving those least disadvantaged, who need only limited preparation before a job can be found for them. There is also the problem of making the punishment fit the crime, and the wrong victims may be punished for ineffective operations. Cleveland researchers queried why a program's needy clients should suffer if their program was discontinued owing to inept administration. Others found that local decisionmakers frequently have shunned high cost activities, supportive services, or especially needy clients because they raised unit costs and thus gave the appearance of poor performance. On the whole, state and local planners have found the selection of evaluation criteria elusive, and a workable system to evaluate manpower programs remains unattainable. Nonethless, the search for "objective" evaluation criteria of social programs appears to have the same fascination as the search for the Holy Grail to the knights of old. The hope that "rigorous" and objective measurements can be bought from modern-day Delphic oracles persists.

A final problem with which state and local planners have grappled is how to link the planning and delivery of services. Even in Cleveland, one of the earliest localities to form a city human resources agency, planning and administration never became effectively coordinated. The city agency was responsible for only a few programs, and the local CAMPS committee was never put under the wing of what central authority existed. In San Diego, ill-feelings developed when program professionals were excluded from the city's planning process. Although CAMPS committees were treated largely as a separate program, it will be impossible for planning and administration to be totally exclusive functions under CETA. Planners now recommend budgets, and both the planning and administrative staffs will work for governors, mayors, or county executives.

What is a "Comprehensive" Program?

Congressional mandates for comprehensive manpower programs existed for almost seven years before CETA was passed. However, instead of using the authority to consolidate local programs that the 1967

Economic Opportunity Act amendments provided in the Comprehensive Work and Training Program, the Labor Department allowed the Concentrated Employment Program to fulfill its obligation. CEP was treated largely as a means of attracting new funds to serve poverty pockets rather than as a way to consolidate existing citywide programs. Only when Congress delayed passage of manpower reform legislation did the Labor Department resurrect the broader CWTP authority and put it to work in pilot "comprehensive" manpower programs.

CEP provided a glimpse into the problems that a so-called comprehensive program was likely to face. Many first-year CETA plans are likely to be modeled after CEPs that contracted directly for a variety of EOA programs to supply training, work experience, and placement services. However, to prevent competition with other agencies which offered parallel manpower services, CEPs were forced to fragment their system by purchasing additional services from other sources. Few CEPs were able to offer their clients employment-related social services which were basic to the concept of serving all their clients' needs. Nonetheless, CEPs had the largest single budget compared with other categorical programs in most cities and some experience in developing formal and informal arrangements with other manpower sponsors.

CETA's consolidation of EOA and MDTA funding under a single prime sponsor solves only some of the problems that CEPs faced. On one hand, it eliminates categorical contracting, an improvement that may not only simplify bookkeeping but more significantly, remove operational rigidities. But, like the CEPs, prime sponsors will be subcontracting with many of the same local agencies—the employment service, vocational institutions, community agencies, business, and labor groups—that made the "old" manpower system appear fragmented and duplicative. Neither can CETA mandate improved relations between the sponsors and employers. And, its budget is too low to enable sponsors to offer all the services they need.

The brief experience of the pilot comprehensive manpower projects, in which Albuquerque pioneered, and of manpower planning councils during the fiscal 1974 planning cycle underlined the CEP experience. They found that once power and funds were fixed in manpower institutions, they were difficult to shift. Improved coordination of individual sponsors and other state, county, or city institutions depended on how far they were willing to go in submitting their planning and management to a confederation of manpower agencies.

While the new law recognizes the benefits of joint planning and coordination of programs, CETA provides for only modest incentives to plan vocational education projects and to establish state manpower councils to promote cooperation between the state agencies and local sponsors. The desirability of linking state agencies and community manpower programs deserves continuing attention, and since one-third of the members of the state manpower services councils will be local officials, mayors and county executives will have an opportunity to air their needs. The training offered by vocational education and rehabilitation programs and the social services available from welfare agencies, for example, could be significant additions to community manpower agencies, enriching and diversifying the services available to enrollees.

It is only a hope that the consolidation of manpower funds under CETA will encourage the state and local sponsors to go even farther than the CEPs did in providing comprehensive manpower services. Judging from their past reluctance to buck the system, it is unrealistic to expect that the new sponsors will test radically new solutions to their manpower problems. Instead, most sponsors will probably feel their way cautiously, gradually giving more of a local tenor to their manpower services.

A Future for Federalism

As a compromise, CETA could only suggest in broad terms the responsibilities and roles of the various government jurisdictions, and the law, therefore, has left nagging questions about the meaning and application of the "New Federalism." Some would have preferred a system that would have been closer to the revenue sharing proposal advanced by the administration in 1971 that required federal funding, but few other federal responsiblities. Congress was not willing, however, to abdicate federal authority and responsibility. It was willing to allow states and communities flexibility in administering their manpower programs, but with adequate federal presence to assure that the goals of the manpower efforts are carried out.

State and local planners and administrators have sounded off from time to time to Congress and the Department of Labor on their needs and recommendations. Like any difficult compromise, CETA was able to incorporate only some of their suggestions. Others found their way into guidelines, and their impact will depend on how federal officials implement the new law. Although crucial, reorganization and improved administration can make only limited contributions to a viable and effective manpower system.

In the final analysis, the level of funding controls the scope of the manpower efforts. Local planners and administrators may debate how to count the needy among residents in their area, but all will agree that their manpower budget is inadequate to meet the needs. A related federal responsibility, and perhaps one that can be more readily undertaken, is longer range funding. Planners have often complained that budget allocations were handed down each spring with planning guidelines, allowing insufficient time to do the nitty gritty of planning before the new fiscal year began. Although CETA's allocation formula must be revised each year and federal budgets are dependent on the legislative process, states and localities have been assured that they will receive at least 90 percent of the previous year's funds.

The budget crunch may also prevent consideration of the soundest recommendations. Manpower officials who seek the opportunity to experiment with program designs not yet tried in the manpower field will find the cupboard bare. But an effective, decentralized manpower system must also guarantee that block grants do not preclude federally supported experimentation with new ideas for planning and delivering manpower services.

Extra money is not the only consideration. Not all manpower programs deserve sustained support, and some should never have been funded. Many have gone through several "versions" and are truly still experiments. For example, some may question, as Albuquerque decisionmakers did, whether the NYC-in-school strategy of "make work" support is appropriate and choose to test more suitable alternatives. Others have suggested the use of vouchers for manpower clients which would allow them to select, as recipients of GI bill benefits do, their own training sites. Such variations are appropriate for experimental and demonstration projects, under which sponsors would not be punished for failure and where the lessons learned could be widely disseminated.

Tight labor markets are no less crucial for the effective operations of manpower programs than increased funds and sustained timely appropriations. During the early 1970s local program agents faced the harsh realities of job shortages in the private sector. The need for better relations with private sector employers was reflected in various measures to motivate employers to cooperate with the manpower system. Several areas planned to link manpower and economic development policies in an attempt to attract new employment opportunities and capture some of the new jobs for manpower clients. Another strategy has been to develop jobs for minority clients to help employers and unions meet equal employment standards. On-the-job training and apprenticeship were considered choice opportunities and both contracted during loose labor markets. Placement of clients in "good" private sector jobs is a continuing need.

More private employment cannot be legislated, and although more money could be appropriated to offer additional inducements to create jobs, significant budgetary boosts are not likely unless unemployment rises. However, requests from state and local planners and administrators that entail limited funds should be heeded by federal officials who have a continuing obligation to help make the new manpower system work.

The funding of training and technical assistance may be a top priority. Capabilities in manpower planning and administrative techniques vary widely. Some areas have proven their expertise; others have gained little sophistication in the manpower arena. A large number of newly endowed county sponsors may be starting from scratch and their technical and administrative capabilities need to be developed. Several have turned to local academic talent, and some help from the staff of the Washington-based public interest groups is available. The feds will likely rely on regional office staff to help state and local sponsors. Whatever the source, more training and technical assistance in labor market data collection and analysis, program evaluation, and administration is one critical commitment that federal policymakers should make in order to smooth the transition to state and local control.

In general, federal technical assistance and guidance is not as objectionable to state and local sponsors as some proponents of the "New Federalism" assert. It is a federal responsibility to guide state and local officials to self-sufficiency in manpower administration, a goal which policymakers have tried to achieve over the past decade. Certainly, where states and localities have gained expertise, they can effectively join federal technicians in assisting less experienced jurisdictions in planning and administering manpower programs.

Decentralization of program administration will affect manpower clients and services marginally, and in some cases not at all. Categorical needs and clients and the proliferation of manpower institutions will not disappear with consolidated funding and public sponsorship. The efficiency and superiority of decategorization remain debatable. And, although the law places state and local governments in the saddle, the issue of who is best suited to sponsor manpower programs is not fully resolved. Different constituencies may be best served by specifically selected institutions, and experience has shown that each will lobby to keep its program alive at the expense of others. Federally determined special claimants of manpower services, like migrant workers and Indians, do not fall conveniently into political jurisdictions, and funding of separate programs may be the only feasible means of assuring that they are served. And many labor markets cross local and state boundaries, leaving some manpower program clients outside the system.

Since manpower programs focus on the needs of a disadvantaged clientele, political accountability by itself may not guarantee that services are provided to those with the least political muscle. Public agencies are often insulated from the wishes of the general public, and decisions on program priorities frequently reflect the values of professional bureaucracies. The manpower system may be more open when public and private sponsors compete to provide services than when entrenched professional bureaucracies are able to maintain tight control over expenditures. CETA retains federally sponsored, categorical programs for special groups and mandates federal responsibilities for research, experimental projects, evaluation, data collection, and overall management of the system. States will exercise little control over the activities of local prime sponsors. Whether this division of authority is optimal will be tested in the coming years. And it is not yet known to what extent the feds will divest themselves of the authority to intervene with state and local manpower plans.

At the federal level, there remains the question of which federal agency should have manpower authority. With CETA, the consolidation of antipoverty manpower programs in the U.S. Department of Labor is far from complete. The U.S. Department of Health, Education, and Welfare will maintain its partnership in the administration of the Work Incentive program and will be the source of funding supportive services. The U. S. Department of Housing and Urban Development retains more than passing interest in manpower issues under the pending community development bill, and the funding of veteran training programs remains completely outside the scope of the U.S. Department of Labor. Programs that may materialize in an effort to meet future economic change may include further duplications of authority. Certainly, shared responsibilities and overlap at the federal level will continue.

From the vantage point of the cities, CETA appeared to give them the independence and flexibility they wanted. The counties were optimistic as well that their needs would be given equitable attention. However, second thoughts about CETA might be expected. The funding retrenchment and uncertain economic conditions have dampened optimism. The fragmentation of labor markets by political jurisdictions is a continuing, although not universal, problem. The states were not in the vanguard championing comprehensive manpower legislation, and whatever interest state spokesmen displayed was apparently generated by dangling the promise of substantial funding. In its final form, CETA, gave the governors less money than they had hoped, direct control only over programs in lesser populated areas, and a weak mandate that they coordinate state and local programs.

CETA suggests a federal system where states and localities would be largely independent of federal controls, where states coordinate statewide programs and the activities of local sponsors, and where the political jurisdictions in local labor markets band together for comprehensive planning and program coordination. However, the promised "comprehensiveness" is left largely to the states and localities to flesh out; federal funds fall far short of the promise.

Notes
Manpower ABCs
Index

Notes

1. Garth L. Mangum, *The Emergency of Manpower Policy* (New York: Holt, Rinehart and Winston, 1969).

2. Howard W. Hallman, Everett Crawford, and Alden Briscoe, *State Manpower Organization* (Washington: Center for Governmental Studies, July 1970), pp. 42-45.

3. U.S., Department of Health, Education, and Welfare, *Digest of Educational Statistics, 1972 Edition* (Washington: Government Printing Office, 1973), Table 23, p. 22; and U.S. Office of Management and Budget, *Special Analyses Budget of the United States, Fiscal Year 1975*, "Special Analysis N: Federal Aid to State and Local Governments" (Washington: Government Printing Office, 1974), Table N-9, pp. 214-217.

4. U.S., Department of Health, Education, and Welfare, *Social Security Bulletin*, 36 (November 1973), Table M-1, p.40.

5. Garth L. Mangum and R. Thayne Robson, ed., *Metropolitan Impact of Manpower Programs: A Four-City Comparison* (Salt Lake City: Olympus Publishing Co., 1973), p. 289.

6. James E. Sawyer, "The State Manpower Planning Council: Utah's Experience," in *Proceedings of National Conference on State and Local Manpower Planning*, ed. by R. Thayne Robson and Garth L. Mangum, Human Resources Institute, University of Utah, April 28-30, 1971, pp. 243-256.

7. Hallman, *State Manpower*, pp. 74-88.

8. National League of Cities/U.S. Conference of Mayors, *Public Employment Program and the Cities*, vol. II, Special Report (Washington: June 19, 1973), p. 12.

9. Sar A. Levitan and Robert Taggart, ed., *Emergency Employment Act: The PEP Generation* (Salt Lake City: The Olympus Publishing Co., 1974).

10. U.S., General Accounting Office, *Study of Federal Programs for Manpower Services for the Disadvantaged in the District of Columbia*, No. B-146879, Washington, D.C., January 30, 1973, p. 3.

11. David Rogers, *Inter-Organizational Relations and Inner City Manpower Programs*, Final Report to the U.S.Department of Labor, Manpower Administration, October 1971, Appendix C, pp. 22-26 and 62-65 (mimeo.).

12. U.S., Department of Labor, *Manpower Report of the President, 1971* (Washington: Government Printing Office, 1971), p. 128.

13. New County, U.S.A. Center, *From America's Counties Today, 1973* (Washington: National Association of Counties, 1973), p. 12.

14. Alfred J. Kahn, *Theory and Practice of Social Planning* (New York: The Russell Sage Foundation, 1969), chap. 12.

15. Alice M. Rivlin, *Systematic Thinking for Social Action* (Washington: The Brookings Institution, 1971), p.3.

16. Garth L. Mangum, *MDTA Foundations of Federal Manpower Policy* (Baltimore: The Johns Hopkins University Press, 1968), pp. 67-72.

17. Stanley H. Ruttenberg, *Manpower Challenge of the 1970's: Institutions and Social Change* (Baltimore: The Johns Hopkins University Press, 1970), p.46.

18. U.S., Department of Health, Education, and Welfare, et.al., *Interagency Cooperative Issuance*, No. 1, March 3, 1967, p. 1.

19. Ruttenberg, *Manpower Challenge of the 1970s*, pp. 50-51.

20. "Statement of Martin L. Peterson, Executive Director, Idaho State Human Resources Development Council," before House Select Subcommittee on Labor, Committee on Education and Labor, *Hearings, Comprehensive Manpower Act of 1973*, 93rd Cong., 1st sess., October 24 and 29, 1973 (Washington: Government Printing Office, 1974), pp. 106-108.

21. John F. Coleman, Alan L. Skvirsky, and Jonathan W. Cox, *A Study of Present Organizational Structure, Relationships and Policies of State and Local CAMPS Organizations,* prepared for the Manpower Administration, U.S. Department of Labor (Washington: Technical Assistance and Training Corp., August 1972), p. 34.

22. James E. Sawyer, *An Assessment of the Objectives and Peformance of a Model State and Local Planning System*, Report to the Office of Research and Development, Manpower Administration, U.S. Department of Labor (Salt Lake City: Olympus Research Corp., November 11, 1973), pp. 64-73.

23. R. Thayne Robson, "The Environment and Perspective of Manpower Planning,"paper delivered at the Pilot Area Manpower Planning Seminar,U.S. Department of Labor, Washington, D.C., April 16-20, 1973, pp. 6-9 (mimeo.).

24. Morris A. Horowitz and Irwin L. Herrnstadt, "The Boston Experience," in Garth L. Mangum and R. Thayne Robson, ed., *Metropolitan Impact of Manpower Programs: A Four-City Comparison*, pp. 86-87.

25. Edward Sofen, "Reflections on the Creation of Miami's Metro," in *Metropolitan Politics,* 2nd ed., ed. by Michael N. Danielson (Boston: Little, Brown and Co., 1971), pp. 285-295.

26. Everett Crawford, Alden F. Briscoe, and Howard W. Hallman, *Metropolitan Manpower Organization* (Washington: Center for Governmental Studies, September 1970), pp. 66-67.

27. Robert A. Aleshire, *Local Planning and Coordination of Manpower Programs* (Washington: National Association for Community Development, 1970), pp. 58-63.

28. James J. Vanecko, *Community Organization in the War on Poverty: An Evaluation of a Strategy for Change in the Community Action Program*

(National Opinion Research Center, The University of Chicago, August, 1970), p. 6.2.

29. James L. Sundquist, *Making Federalism Work* (Washington: The Brookings Institution, 1969), pp. 39-40.

30. Howard W. Hallman, *Community Control* (Washington: Washington Center for Metropolitan Studies, 1969), pp. 135-164.

31. George J. Washnis, *Model Cities Impact on Better Communities*, prepared for the Subcommittee on Housing of the House Committee on Banking and Currency, 93rd Cong., 1st sess. (Washington: Government Printing Office, December 1973).

32. John H. Strange, "Citizen Participation in Community Action and Model Cities Programs," *Public Administration Review*, Special Issue, 32 (October 1972), pp. 661-662.

33. U.S., Congress, Senate, *Examination of the War on Poverty, Part 10, Hearings* before the Subcommittee on Employment, Manpower and Poverty of the Committee on Labor and Public Welfare, 90th Cong., 1st sess. (Washington: Government Printing Office, July 10, 13, and 18, 1967), pp. 3308-3315.

34. U.S., Congress, Senate, *Economic Opportunity Amendments of 1969, Hearings* before the Subcommittee on Employment, Manpower and Poverty of the Committee on Labor and Public Welfare, 91st Cong., 1st sess. (Washington: Government Printing Office, June 5, 1969), p. 483.

35. U.S., Department of Labor, *Manpower Report of the President, 1967* (Washington: Government Printing Office, 1967), pp. 74-75.

36. Camil Associates, Inc., *Evaluation of Supportive Services Provided for Participants of Manpower Programs,* Final Report to U.S. Department of Labor, Manpower Administration, September 30, 1972, pp. 9-12 (mimeo.).

37. Peter Kobrak, "The Role of American Business in Urban Manpower Programs: Divergent Orientations of Community Power and Service Organizations in the Manpower Game," paper delivered at the 1971 Annual Meeting of the American Political Science Association, Chicago, Ill., September 7-11, 1971, p. 27 (mimeo.).

38. U.S., Department of Labor, *Manpower Report of the President, March 1974*, Table F-1 and Office of Financial and Management Information Systems, "CEP-Program Data Summary," August 10, 1973 (mimeo.).

39. U.S., General Accounting Office, *Review of Economic Opportunity Act Programs*, No. B-130515, March 18, 1969, printed for the use of the Senate Committee on Labor and Public Welfare and the House Committee on Education and Labor, 91st Cong., 1st sess. (Washington: Government Printing Office, 1969), pp. 45-50.

40. Camil Associates, Inc., *Evaluation of Supportive Services Provided for Participants of Manpower Programs*, pp. A24-A26.

41. Systems Development Corporation, *Analysis of the Concentrated Employment Program Subsequent to Manpower Administration Order 14-69,*

prepared for the Office of Policy, Evaluation, and Research, Manpower Administration, U.S. Department of Labor, pp. 97-102 (mimeo.).

42. U.S., Department of Labor, Manpower Administration, Office of Financial and Management Information Systems, "CEP-Program Data Summary," August 10, 1973 (mimeo.).

43. U.S., Department of Labor, Manpower Administration, *Order No. 14-69,* "Refunding of CEP I and II Programs," July 19, 1969, Attachment 2, p. 7 (mimeo.).

44. U.S., Congress, Senate, *Manpower Development and Training Legislation, 1970, Hearings* before the Subcommittee on Employment, Manpower, and Poverty of the Committee on Labor and Public Welfare, 91st Cong., 1st and 2nd sess. (Washington: Government Printing Office, November 4 and 5, 1969), pp. 193-194.

45. Camil Associates, Inc., *Evaluation of Supportive Services Provided for Participants of Federal Manpower Programs,* pp. 8-9.

46. Roger H. Davidson, *The Politics of Comprehensive Manpower Legislation* (Baltimore: The Johns Hopkins University Press, 1972), pp. 10-11.

47. U.S., Congress, House, "Supplemental Appropriations Bill, 1973," *Report from the Committee on Appropriations,* No. 92-1555, 92nd Cong., 2nd sess. (Washington: Government Printing Office, October 10, 1972), pp. 13-14.

48. Howard W. Hallman, *Pilot Comprehensive Manpower Program: Implications of Its Experience for Local and State Manpower Organization,* prepared for the U.S. Department of Labor, Manpower Administration, October 1973, pp. 19-95 (mimeo.).

49. William Lilley III, Timothy B. Clark, and John K. Iglehard, "New Federalism II/Planned Variations," *National Journal,* 5 (March 3, 1973), p. 297.

50. Robert Guttman, "The Comprehensive Employment and Training Act," Congressional Research Service, Library of Congress, March 5, 1974, pp. 3-4 (processed).

51. Jon H. Goldstein, "The Effectiveness of Manpower Training Programs: A Review of Research on the Impact of the Poor," *Studies in Public Welfare,* Paper No. 3, prepared for the Subcommittee on Fiscal Policy of the Joint Economic Committee, 92nd cong., 2nd sess. (Washington: Government Printing Office, November 20, 1972).

Manpower ABCs

ARA	Area Redevelopment Act of 1961
AVA	American Vocational Association
BAT	Bureau of Apprenticeship and Training
BES	Bureau of Employment Security
BWTP	Bureau of Work Training Programs
CAA	Community Action Agency
CAMPS	Cooperative Area Manpower Planning System
CAP	Community Action Program
CDA	City Demonstration Agency
CEP	Concentrated Employment Program
CETA	Comprehensive Employment and Training Act of 1973
CMP	Comprehensive Manpower Program
COG	Council of Governments
CWTP	Comprehensive Work and Training Program
EDT	Employability Development Team
EEA	Emergency Employment Act of 1971
EOA	Economic Opportunity Act of 1964
HEW	U.S. Department of Health, Education, and Welfare
HRD	Human Resources Development
HUD	U.S. Department of Housing and Urban Development
JOBS	Job Opportunities in the Business Sector
MDTA	Manpower Development and Training Act of 1962
NAB	National Alliance of Businessmen
NACo	National Association of Counties
NGC	National Governors' Conference
NLC/USCM	National League of Cities/U.S. Conference of Mayors
NYC	Neighborhood Youth Corps
OEO	Office of Economic Opportunity
OIC	Opportunities Industrialization Center
OJT	On-the-job Training
OMAT	Office of Manpower Automation and Training
OMB	Office of Management and Budget
OPER	Office of Policy, Evaluation and Research

PEP	Public Employment Program
PSC	Public Service Careers
SER	Service, Employment, Redevelopment
SMSA	Standard Metropolitan Statistical Area
USES	United States Employment Service
WIN	Work Incentive Program

Index

Action for Boston Community Development, Inc. (ABCD), 27, 30, 71-72, 76

AFL-CIO, 42; Human Resources Development Institutes (HRDI), 35

Albuquerque Office of Manpower Programs, 71; agreement with CAA, 65-66

Allowances, 36; under CETA, 37

American Vocational Association (AVA), 42

Apprenticeship: apprenticeship councils, 21; apprenticeship outreach programs, 35

Area Redevelopment Act (ARA) of 1961, 1

Assistant regional directors for manpower (ARDMs), 17, 18

Better Communities Act, 79

Block grants, 12, 115

Bureau of Employment Security (BES), 15-16, 49, 51. See also U.S. Employment Service

California Department of Employment Development (DED): in San Diego, 29-30

California Department of Human Resources Development, 22

Categorical grants, 11-12, 31, 67

City demonstration agencies (CDA), 77. See also Model Cities

Cleveland AIM-JOBS, 84-85

Cleveland Department of Human Resources and Economic Development (DHRED), 38-39

Community action agencies (CAA): in the District of Columbia, 30; and manpower programs, 30-31, 75-76; in Boston, 30, 76, 108; and manpower planning, 65-66; impact of 1967 EOA amendments on, 76-77, 80; planning in, 77; contributions of, 77, 79-80; future of, 77, 105; and CWTP, 80-81

Community Action Program (CAP), 2, 75. See also Community action agencies

Comprehensive Employment and Training Act (CETA) of 1973: passage of, iv, v, 8; congressional jurisdiction, 8; alternatives to, 8-10; consolidation of programs, 8, 31-32, 103, 113-114, 116-117; vocational education incentives, 10, 42, 97, 99, 114; planning under, 10, 53, 72-73; impact on the employment service, 20; impact on state agencies, 22, 98-99, 114; state manpower services councils, 24, 55, 56, 98-99; role of governors, 24, 98-99, 104; public employment provisions, 34, 99-100, 106; sponsors, 52, 61, 106; incentives for multijurisdictional arrangements, 52, 64, 98, 110-111; data collection mandates, 58, 101-102, 111; redistribution of funds, 61; provisions for planning council representation, 64; goal of comprehensive programs, 74; and intergovernmental relations, 96, 103, 118; funding recommenda-